First Additions

Strategies for Adding On

First Additions

Strategies for Adding On

Stuart Cohen and Julie Hacker

Introduction by Steven W. Semes

Contents

Preface

"...it follows that one whose knowledge of science is purely theoretical is usually a pretty clumsy fellow, while an artist whose knowledge of science is only practical is but a very limited craftsman."
—Denis Diderot (1751)

"...theory, if not rightly received at the door of an empirical discipline, comes in through the chimney like a ghost and upsets the furniture."
—Irwin Panofsky (1955)

This book is intended to document an architectural practice. It presents in writing and photographs a theoretical position and resultant architectural strategies for making additions to existing buildings. While the illustrations in this book are residential, we believe these principles extend to existing commercial and institutional structures as well. Some of the additions illustrated are small but we hope they have had a transformative impact; often the smallest projects are the most challenging.

After a decade of doing house additions in the 1970s and 1980s, the conceit that our practice, then Stuart and Anders Nereim, was "idea driven," led to Stuart Cohen's article in 1985, called "On Adding On" (Thresholds 1985, pp75-90). This book includes a reprint of "On Adding On" and a second new essay, "In What Style Shall We Build," addressing the question of the architectural language of an addition. Together these two essays describe the ideas illustrated in the work of Cohen & Hacker Architects.

Few of the additions that we have been asked to do have been large enough or important enough, in our opinion, to warrant employing a fully independent extension strategy or a visually different architectural language. Instead, we will often transform either detailed elements or compositional strategies to subtly announce our presence. "In What Style Shall We Build" argues that the choice of a visual language should be based on the perceived hierarchy of an addition relative to the original structure.

"On Adding On" purported to be neutral with respect to the choice of an architectural vocabulary even though the additions illustrated were mostly examples showing buildings extended using the forms and details of the original structures. What was missing were reasons for when to extend and utilize the architectural language of the original building and when an addition in a different style might be appropriate. Requiring an addition to be in the style of the original building, it is often argued, inhibits the originality and creativity of the architect. The most well-known contradiction of this assertion is to be found in the architectural works of Michelangelo. These were entirely additions and remodeling of existing buildings. All were transformative not only of the existing buildings but of the language of Classical architecture.

Introduction Steven W. Semes

Some years ago, then Prince Charles, who at the time was royal patron of the Society for the Protection of Ancient Buildings—a leading architectural conservation organization in the United Kingdom, also known as SPAB— was invited to write a foreword to a book to be published by SPAB as a manual for restoring old houses.[1] The future King suggested in his draft that an insistence on using design and materials of one's own time for new or added work had been used too often to justify unsatisfactory alterations and ugly additions. At a time when current fashion in design was conspicuously oppositional to historic architecture, it was better, he felt, to restore buildings in their original style rather than impose on them alien forms and materials. This statement was unacceptable to SPAB, which saw it as violating its core principles enshrined in the 1877 "Manifesto" of its founder, William Morris.[2] SPAB had, for many decades, encouraged the use of modern architecture and materials when adding to or altering historic buildings. When SPAB rejected Charles's text, the Prince withdrew from the project and resigned as its patron.

Those who have not done business with professionals or academics in historic preservation might be surprised to learn that opinions on the subject of the appropriate way to add to old houses or buildings are so sharply contested that even the heir to the British throne can be rebuffed for holding the "wrong" views. Most of the public appears to support Charles's approach, but mainstream historic preservation professionals tend to find any recourse to historic forms, styles, or materials inappropriate when adding to a historic structure or designing infill in a historic district. Additions to historic sites, they will say, must represent "the architecture of our time" and provide a clear visual distinction between historic material and new elements. The public and the preservation elite have been split on this issue at least since the 1960s.

As the authors of this book point out in their essay "In What Style Shall We Build?" the underlying assumption is that contemporary and historic architecture are inherently opposed and should remain distinct. Typically, contemporary architects designing a substantial addition to an existing building will view their new part as challenging or confronting the historic part. What might appear to be a stylistic prejudice, however, is justified by the supposed need for legibility—allowing observers to trace the historical development of a structure by identifying the times when different parts were constructed. Alternatively, an addition will seek to join the preexisting building to form a larger whole using style, scale, and deference to draw them together. These more contextual projects will generally find favor with neighbors and the general public but may be questioned by the local design review authorities who might label such designs "historicist" or "pastiche."

This debate is nothing new. As the authors retrace in their essay, the arguments extend back into the nineteenth century when the English School of conservation, led by John Ruskin and William Morris, limited preservation treatments to "pure conservation" without restoration or reconstruction of decayed or missing elements and additions were to be clearly identifiable as such. It was the heirs of these two thinkers who rejected the then Prince of Wales's forward. Opposing them was the French School, led by Eugène Emmanuel Viollet-le-Duc and his followers, who sought stylistic unity through the addition of new elements designed to join the historic ones seamlessly, as if the original designers had returned to make the additions themselves. In the twentieth century, an Italian School led by Camillo Boito and Gustavo Giovannoni sought a middle ground between the English and French approaches, recognizing that each had something positive to offer as well as errors to be avoided. For example, they thought, the former could lead to an unrealistic preference for the ruin, while the latter might result in counterfeits.

These debates continue today, reflected in official guidance for historic preservation work. SPAB, for example, still requires new members to sign Morris's 1877 Manifesto as a kind of loyalty oath. There is no question that SPAB's approach is the predominant one internationally, though the French and Italian attitudes continue to be a significant minority. The ICOMOS Venice Charter of 1964, a key document in international preservation guidance, requires that new elements "depart from the original composition and bear a contemporary stamp."[3] In the United States, the Secretary of the Interior's Standards for Rehabilitation, first issued in 1977, require that the "new work shall be differentiated from the old and shall be compatible with the massing, size, scale, and architectural features to protect the historic integrity of the property and its environment."[4]

In theory, it is sensible to ask added elements to appear as such, but in practice, this requirement presents some difficulties. First, while contemporary architectural fashions, with their intentional transgression of the underlying principles and forms of traditional architecture, make it easy to "differentiate" new forms from the historic ones, they do not offer many tools for exhibiting "compatibility." Contemporary architects and design review boards often consider the criterion of "compatibility" met by making the new addition, however discordant in appearance it may be, the same size as the historic building it joins or lining up horizontal elements—cornice lines and window sills—across the elevations. This, at least, has the merit of seeming objective, if leaving the essential oxymoronic requirements unresolved. Second, while a first addition might follow the path of "differentiation," what about a second or a third addition? If those must also be differentiated from the original structure and previous additions, the maintenance of historic character over time would seem impossible—surely a counterproductive preservation outcome.

One of the central tenets of the Italian School was that new work should be identifiable but that "differentiation" should be subtle, allowing the new and the old together to constitute a visual whole. Distinguishing the new from the old allows observers to understand the historical development of the site, however that distinction should not create unnecessary dissonance between new and old. This viewpoint has found new support in recent decades, as in the ICOMOS Valletta Principles of 2011:

Regardless of style and expression, all new architecture should avoid the negative effects of drastic or excessive contrasts and of fragmentation and interruptions in the continuity of the urban fabric and space. Priority must be given to a continuity of composition that does not adversely affect the existing architecture but at the same time allows a discerning creativity that embraces the spirit of the place.[5]

While "continuity of composition" and "discerning creativity" seem as rare as ever, alternatives are increasingly visible and this is where the present book comes in with its documentation of Cohen and Hacker 's efforts over several decades to establish an equilibrium between continuity and creativity. While simply reproducing historic detail or imposing a different modern style are both relatively easy for the architect, finding a balance that fulfills equally the criteria of "differentiation" and "compatibility" is quite difficult in practice. It gets easier if the architect no longer feels compelled to impose stylistic contrast as a means of "differentiating" the new elements from historic fabric. Freed from ideological preconceptions, the designer finds a range of different responses and a new freedom to respond appropriately.

The projects collected here, though not necessarily involving officially designated historic properties, show us how the sensitivity one would expect of an architect adding on to a valued protected site might also be applied to a project involving a more ordinary preexisting condition—such as an unremarkable suburban house without any kind of historic preservation regulation. Why wouldn't a project to enlarge the existing house merit the same search for a balance between respecting the context and introducing new elements and characters? This is not a case of uncritical imitation, but choosing the formal expression from a spectrum of possibilities ranging from literal reproduction to intentional opposition.[6] The projects illustrated here reveal a greater or lesser "literalness" in the degree to which the new appears continuous with the preexisting work. In some cases, "differentiation" is emphasized, in others "compatibility," but they all seek a balance arrived at on a case-by-case basis grounded in an understanding of the context.

Designing an addition to an existing piece of architecture, even one humble in character or modest in scale, is like entering a social event already in progress—perhaps an elegant reception. I see that I do not know anyone there, but I cautiously approach one group engaged in conversation, listen for some minutes to understand what they are talking about, nod my head occasionally, and gradually join the conversation, adding my point of view, and maybe even changing the subject if I do so with tact. Anything else will probably end the conversation and ensure I am not invited back to similar events in the future.

Architectural additions are similarly exercises in social grace requiring tact and respect. Our beautiful historic places were produced by an extended series of such sensitive additions based on the premise that maintaining the architectural character of the place as a whole is more important than reflecting the date of construction of any one structure or promoting a particular contemporary style. Even formal opposition is welcome when the context demands it. The examples discussed in the authors' essay "On Adding On," show us the way to that "continuity of composition" and "discerning creativity" requested by the Valletta Principles. This approach, applicable to cities as well as to houses, allows us to conserve our architectural inheritance and add to it in ways that make our valued places more beautiful, sustainable, and just.

Steven W. Semes practiced architecture in Washington, D.C., San Francisco, and New York for nearly 30 years before joining the faculty of the University of Notre Dame in 2005. Since 2022, he has been the Director of the Michael Christopher Duda Center for Preservation, Resilience, and Sustainability at the School of Architecture there. He is the author of *The Architecture of the Classical Interior and The Future of the Past: A Conservation Ethic for Architecture, Urbanism, and Historic Preservation* as well as many articles. He is translator and co-editor of the forthcoming book, *New Building in Old Cities: Writings of Gustavo Giavannoni on Architectural and Urban Conservation.* His current research focuses on the issue of defining appropriate new architecture in historic settings.

NOTES

[1] Blakely, Kennedy, and Dora Kennedy. Architect's Journal. "Prince Charles Quites Heritage Society in Censorship Row." July 13, 2009. https://www.architectsjournal.co.uk/archive/prince-charles-quits-heritage-society-in-censorship-row.

[2] Morris, William, Philip Webb, et al. The Society for the Protection of Ancient Buildings. "The SPAB Manifesto." 1877. https://www.spab.org.uk/about-us/spab-manifesto.

[3] International Council on Monuments and Sites. "International Charter for the Conservation and Restoration of Monuments and Sites (The Venice Charter)." 1965. https://www.icomos.org/en/participer/179-articles-en-francais/ressources/charters-and-standards/157-thevenice-charter.

[4] The National Park Service. "The Secretary of the Interior's Standards for Rehabilitation." 1977. https://www.nps.gov/subjects/taxincentives/secretarys-standards-rehabilitation.htm.

[5] International Council on Monuments and Sites. "The Valletta Principles for the Safeguarding and Management of Historic Cities, Towns, and Urban Areas." 2011. https://civvih.icomos.org/wp-content/uploads/2022/03/Valletta-Principles-GA-_EN_FR_28_11_2011.pdf.

[6] Semes, Steven W. *The Future of the Past: A Conversation Ethic for Architecture, Urbanism, and Historic Preservation.* New York: W. W. Norton & Co., 2009.

Revisiting "On Adding On"

The historian Anthony Alofsin once said of the prolific author Frank Lloyd Wright that writing was for him, "... a vehicle to sort out and through his ideas...Books and articles could circulate buildings rested in place." For many architects, analysis and synthesis are reciprocal processes in making architecture. Writing not only clarifies ideas but can codify them. "On Adding On," published in a 1985 edition of *Thresholds,* the Journal of the school of architecture at the University of Illinois Chicago, served that purpose. An important influence at the time was Michael Graves' 1975 article in the *Journal of Architectural Education,* called the "Swedish Connection." In it, he describes a studio problem he taught at Princeton University which asked students to add on to the 1918 Snellman House built by the Swedish architect Gunnar Asplund. In his article, Graves suggests that a strategy for making additions is to think of the original building as an incomplete "fragment" and to image an addition as a completion of that "fragment." This suggests an extrapolation of both the plan organization, the compositional ideas of the building's massing and openings, and even the idea of the addition as a recall or a play on the original building's architectural language. Graves recalled that many of his students designed additions to the front of the house that tried to resolve the

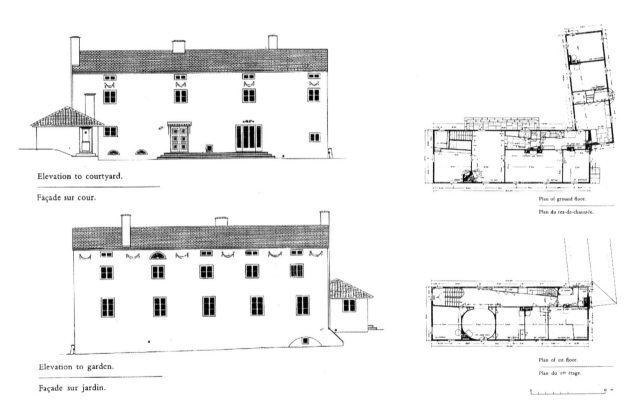

Elevation to courtyard.

Façade sur cour.

Elevation to garden.

Façade sur jardin.

Plan of ground floor.

Plan du rez-de-chaussée.

Plan of 1st floor.

Plan du 1er étage.

Snellman House. Gunnar Asplund, architect. Djursholm, Stockholm, Sweden. 1918.

compositional duality of the entry doors and the French doors out from the living room to the same raised entry terrace. This suggests that additions might also be thought of as "corrections," which was the interpretation of the south half of Chicago's Monadnock building suggested in "On Adding On."

While Graves would later come to national prominence for his postmodern buildings and his product designs, the implication of his article seemed to be disconnected from his work of the same period. The "Swedish Connection" was a mindset to establish a starting point for a design rather than an actual strategy. Most additions are either pavilions or extensions of an existing building. Even vertical and concentric additions are forms of extension. This was the thesis of "On Adding On" which illustrated these categories with both historic and contemporary examples.

The second impetus for this article was the idea of contextualism, formulated as an urban design strategy at Cornell University in the 1960s and '70s in the Master of Architecture program in Urban Design, taught by Colin Rowe. This strategy did not address the design of new cities but adding to or infilling areas of existing ones. The characteristics—street grid, geometry, and building types—of the existing urban context were taken as a starting point in design. As a strategy, contextualism seemed equally applicable to architectural design. This was suggested in Cohen's 1974 article, "Physical Context, Cultural Context, Including It All" in the second issue of *Oppositions,* the journal of the Institute for Architecture and Urban Studies in New York, which existed from 1967 to 1984. We believed that these ideas also applied to the design of building additions. The existing building is the context. Choosing the context as a starting point requires a conscious value judgement. This judgement is the acceptance or rejection of the existing conditions. An alternative to blindly accepting the context and simply replicating it was the idea that an addition could be a commentary or criticism of the original building or an attempt at its transformation, an idea also explored briefly in "On Adding On."

On Adding On
by Stuart Cohen (Reprinted from *Thresholds,* 1985)

The existing order is complete before the new work arrives; for it to persist after the supervention of novelty, the whole existing order must be, if ever so slightly altered, and so the relations, proportions, values of each work of art towards the whole are readjusted; and this is conformity between the old and the new. Whoever has approved this idea of order ... will not find it preposterous that the past should be altered by the present as much as the present is directed by the past.

—T.S. Eliot [1]

Eliot's words describe a reciprocal relationship he perceives between new and existing works of art. For him, the meaning of the new work is always found through its relationship to an existing frame of reference. In contemporary architectural theory this idea is reflected in contextualism. While the literature of contextualism has dealt predominantly with urban design, the architectural issue of the relationship of new construction to existing buildings is seen most clearly in the problem of the building addition.

By an addition we shall mean new construction (not rebuilding or remodeling) which is added to an existing structure by being physically attached to it. This eliminates ensembles and complexes of buildings as well as cities from consideration, although these are often useful models, having grown over time by an additive process.

Additions are made to buildings to alter their function or their perception, to increase their usable space, or to change their appearance in relation to a new use or current architectural style. An example which embodies all of these would be the rebuilding of basilican churches such as St. Maria Maggiore in Rome. Here the physical size of the church was increased, its internal spatial configuration was modified in relation to changes in liturgy, and its exterior was totally altered to "modernize" its appearance.

Historically, additions to existing structures have been significant building commissions. The completion of St. Peter's and the Vatican comprised a sequence of additions. Likewise, the Louvre evolved to its present form and function through a series of additions completed when Visconti, followed by Lufuel in the 1850s and 60s, added a new wing and effectively adjusted the building's geometry so as to terminate the axis of the Champs Elysees.

In the past, the problem of the building addition was frequently part of a program calling for the transformation of an entire structure. On the Capitoline Hill, Michelangelo's additions completely altered the fronts of all three existing buildings, eliminating any problem of juxtaposition between new and old architectural styles (Figs. 1, 2). If Michelangelo's transformation of the Capitoline represents one extreme, the opposite might be illustrated by the Villa Giulia outside of Rome (Fig. 3). Because of the circumstances of its design and construction, the villa was the result of an additive process. The formal integration of its parts was so skillful that it created a confusion as to their exact authorship which has been commented on by John Coolidge: "According to writers of the period the Pope asked several different designers to collaborate on the building. The papal courtiers were notoriously meddlesome, and the Pope himself was fickle, which led to a constant changing of the plans. What resulted, in fact, was an elaborate palimpsest, a series of superimposed projects, each one partially carried out and then in part replaced by later schemes ... so that the various sections they designed are not readily distinguishable. The separate layers of the palimpsest melt into one another before the baffled eyes of the modern student. "[2] Historians have acknowledged the difficulty of distinguishing the part played by Vignola from that of Ammannati, Sansovino, Vasari, and even Michelangelo. Where each artist might have chosen to ignore or destroy the work of a prior architect, the circumstances of the commission, along with a shared formal vocabulary, produced work of remarkable continuity. Between the extremes of the Villa Giulia, where everything was retained, and the Capitoline, where a totally new entity was created, lies a wide range of possibilities. Each extreme and its modification by degrees is valid when in support of an appropriate meaning for the building and its addition.

The examples of the Capitoline and the Villa Giulia consider only the appearance of the respective additions. This is only one aspect of how we understand architectural meaning. Meaning is also conveyed by the formal relationship of the addition to the original structure. This relationship may be seen in both the organization of the elements of the addition and in its location and connection to the existing structure. In considering building additions, these factors need to be examined jointly with emphasis on the way additions form a hierarchy of perceived importance with the other parts of a building.

Fig. 1. *View of the Capitoline Hill, Rome, c. 1554-1560.*

Fig. 2. *Michelangelo, Capitoline Hill, Rome.*

Fig. 3. *Villa Giulia, Rome.*

All building additions are of two basic types which we shall call *conjunctive* and *disjunctive.* These terms were selected to suggest the perceived relationship of the added part to both the original structure and the new complex. Conjunctive additions are visually integrated with the original building and may or may not be identifiable. Disjunctive additions retain their discrete identity. Whether an addition is conjunctive or disjunctive is simultaneously a function of its formal organization, size, and architectural elements as they relate to the original. The function, purpose, and symbolic meaning of the addition, in relationship to the other parts of the building, should determine its appropriate degree of articulation or visual uniqueness—whether the addition should be conjunctive or disjunctive.

Conjunctive additions are usually contiguous with an existing building and are usually an extension of the formal organization and the architectural elements of the original. Conjunctive additions are, by definition, dependent on the existence of the original structure and are hierarchically less important except when the only other determinant of importance is size. Conjunctive additions are appropriate when an addition should be equal to or less important than the original structure. This includes most building additions, particularly those where the addition exists primarily to enlarge a building's useable space.

Disjunctive additions are visually or physically discontinuous with the original building. They may be either visually complete and independent or visually incomplete and dependent on the original structure. When conceived as physically independent of the original structure they may still be functionally, programmatically, or symbolically dependent on it. Disjunctive additions usually have a high relative importance. When they are articulated from the original structure this importance will result from the constancies of perception which place primary importance on figures over grounds. Disjunctive additions are appropriate when an addition should be equal to or more important than the original structure. A chapel or shrine, an auditorium or other place of assembly, a president's or director's office, a treasury, a special collections room at a museum, or a rare book room at a library would all be appropriate examples of disjunctive additions.

The categories of conjunctive and disjunctive refer to our perception of the addition. These correspond in a general way to two sets of strategies for the physical relationship of the addition to the original building. These strategies are addition by extension or by the creation of a new *discrete structure.*

Additions to buildings that are extensions usually continue the form, formal organization, or architectural elements of the original. These extensions may be lateral, frontal, concentric, or vertical. Extensions which utilize the same architectural elements as the original building tend to be conjunctive. Those utilizing dissimilar elements will be disjunctive except for extensions which are symmetrical about the original building. These tend to be conjunctive, independent of their architectural elements.

Concentric extensions of a building are a special category of symmetrical extensions. They may be conjunctive or disjunctive depending on the relationship of the addition to its center. If the addition is part of the same formal system and uses the same architectural elements, it will be conjunctive and the central structure may lose its identity as a figure. If the addition is disjunctive and part of a different formal system, it may function as a ground allowing the continued identity and dominance of the central figure.

Extensions may also be completions of an existing structure if it is incomplete or they may transform an already complete building into a new entity. Additions which are completions depend on the perception of the original building as incomplete. In "The Swedish Connection," an article by Michael Graves on building additions, Graves proposes "completions" as a category or type of addition.[3] He suggests that a starting point for approaching any addition might be the assumption that the existing building can be perceived as an "incomplete fragment" of a larger whole. This proposition seems clear when a building configuration is asymmetrical or actually incomplete. When it is not, a new configuration must be conceived, of which the original building can become a part.

Additions which are discrete structures, or "pavilionized," will always be disjunctive except when they are paired and bilaterally symmetrical in their form, organization, and location with respect to the existing structure. This special condition may be thought of as a type of completion. Disjunctive additions which are discrete structures are, by definition, always linked to the original building. Conceptually, the link joining the two structures may be a solid or a void. The solid link may be conceived as an extension of the architectural elements and formal organization of either the original structure or its addition. As such, it can function to establish a relationship between the architectural elements of the two structures if they have been contrasted, or it can establish a scale relationship when the parts being joined are vastly dissimilar in size. The linking element conceived as a solid may also be a third, independent element (such as the vertically articulated corner pavilions that connect the wings of the Louvre). The linking element conceived as a void has its origins in the open arbor, covered arcade, glass enclosed porches, and conservatories that often joined pavilions and out-buildings to a principal structure. Modern architecture conceived of the glass link as invisible; a literal void. This is never the case. As the size of the link is compressed, the linking void is reduced to a line of intersection between the new and old structure with nothing to resolve the juxtaposition between visually dissimilar architectural elements.

We have identified some of the properties of conjunctive and disjunctive additions as a function of their formal organization and choice of architectural elements. These properties may also be a function of the compositional modes of certain architectural styles. The disjunction usually created by dissimilar forms, materials, and details will not always occur when an addition is made to a building whose style and compositional strategies are asymmetric or picturesque.[4]

Thus far, the meaning of an addition as a function of its visual relationship to the original structure, determined by the correct hierarchy of all the parts of the building based on function and purpose, has been considered. Meaning may be predetermined by other considerations. Meaning in architecture serves in part as a method of explaining the world—making it comprehensible by giving it shape and boundaries, and defining our place in it. If architecture can take on this function by virtue of its relationship to its surroundings, then the building addition in turn can take on the task of explaining or clarifying the building to which it is added. In this sense, additions may be thought of as a form of criticism,[5] since criticism, according to T.S. Eliot, " ... must always profess an end in view, which, roughly speaking, appears to be the elucidation of works of art and the correction of taste."[6]

Architecture as criticism may constitute a social or cultural criticism, a physical criticism of contemporary architectural style, or a criticism of an immediate physical context. As recent architectural histories have pointed out, all of these criticisms were explicit in the forms, symbolic content, and social programs of modern architecture. With respect to building additions, the tenets of modernism dictated the articulation of an addition as a discretely identifiable part. In this way the discrimination of the new from the old could communicate modern architecture's belief in the renewal of society through building.

This was the intended reading of the contrast between the original and the addition. Thus, the addition was offered as a model for the reconstruction of the whole.

If an object of criticism is elucidation, it may be accomplished by comparison, contrast (the comparison of differences), and interpretation. This suggests a role for additions in which they can serve as a commentary on an existing building, its architectural elements, style, meaning, and merit as a work of art. This can be accomplished through the repetition of selected forms, details, and compositional themes to focus attention on their role in the original; the creation of a miniature which, because of its size, can be grasped at once allowing us to more completely understand the form and organization of the original; the abstraction or; transformation of elements from the original; and the use of "collaged" elements taken from an entirely different visual system and set in contrast to the corresponding elements of the original. Thus, most additions would seem to contain elements of criticism of the original structure, so that, intended or unintended, each addition may be seen as a value judgement—a positive or negative criticism—of the building to which it is added. With these issues of addition in mind we might examine a selection of specific examples. Rather than trying to systematically illustrate categories of addition strategies, it may be more interesting to look at how the variables of strategy and the choice of specific architectural elements affect the perception of an enlarged building.

Fig. 4. *Louis Sullivan, Carson Pirie Scott Store, Chicago, 1906.*

We might begin by looking at two historically important Chicago buildings, both of which came to their present configurations through major additions which were extensions. In both additions the choice of specific architectural elements reflects a value judgement about the architectural merit of the original building. In 1891, the dry goods firm of Schlessinger and Mayer hired Adler and Sullivan to design an addition to their original building at the corner of State and Madison Streets and to redesign the exterior to give a unified appearance to the structure. This commission was never carried out, in part because of the depression of 1893. In 1899, Schlessinger and Mayer decided to build a new building at this location and hired Sullivan, who had dissolved his partnership with Adler. Their new building and the sequence by which it was enlarged is described by Carl Condit (Fig. 4): "The new 1899 structure was three bays wide and nine stories high and stood on Madison Street somewhat east of the intersection with State. It constituted the first portion of the present Carson Pirie Scott Store."

In 1903, the old building at the corner and its neighbor immediately to the south were demolished, and, in the same year, Sullivan designed the extension of the original Madison Street building. This addition, twelve stories high and consisting of three bays along Madison and seven along State, was built between 1903 and 1904. In the latter year Carson, Pirie, Scott and Company bought the business from Schlessinger and Mayer. In 1906, D.H. Burnham and Company were commissioned to design the last addition of the original group, the five south bays on State Street which were constructed in the same year. Burnham wisely elected to follow Sullivan's plans in every detail except in the treatment of the top story. Thus the completed building-six bays on Madison and twelve on State-emerged in steps. It remained unchanged until 1948, when the original cornice or roof projection was replaced by a parapet."[7] As Condit points out, only the windows of the top floor of Burnham's addition originally indicated the point at which his addition began. In 1948, when the cornice was removed, these windows were altered, further unifying the two structures. Sullivan's famous corner entrance, because it avoided the problem of establishing a center for the long State Street facade, made the building's extension a simple proposition. Burnham and Company designed a lateral extension using identical architectural elements. It was completely dependent on and integrated into the form of the original structure.

Fig. 5. *Holabird & Roche, Monadnock Building Addition, Chicago, 1893.*

The Monadnock Building, a long narrow office structure fronting on Jackson and Dearborn Streets in Chicago, was also the result of two successive construction projects. The building was commissioned by the Brooks family of Boston, the same clients who had commissioned many of Burnham and Root's other Chicago office buildings. The building was conceived and built in two halves, the north half designed by John Root and known as the Monadnock and Kearsage building, and the south half known as the Katahdin, designed by Holabird and Roche (Fig. 5). The building was a joint investment by different members of the Brooks family and was designed so that it could be subdivided into independent portions for separate operation and even separate sale. The north half, designed by Root, was built as a masonry bearing wall structure because his conservative clients did not believe that the new method of steel frame construction created a truly permanent structure. The south addition was built with a steel frame for economic reasons. John Root's Monadnock Building has been lauded for its strong form and daring elimination of ornament, while Holabird and Roche's structure has been largely overlooked. Yet it was a brilliant addition to Root's building. It was a lateral extension which repeated the forms and materials of the north half as a device to visually integrate the two structures, while introducing an entirely different visual language. In Root's structure, the bay windows warped forward as an extension of the building's masonry surface, with the bearing wall between them accentuated by deep window reveals. In the Holabird and Roche addition, the verticals of the structural frame were given continuous expression with the bays appearing to weave in and out behind them. Where Root's building was devoid not only of ornament but of the elements of a correct architectural style, the Holabird and Roche addition incorporated a three-story base with a giant order of classical piers more in scale with the size of the building than Root's one-story base. The addition also had an attic story differentiated by a change in fenestration and terminated by a classical cornice. The incorporation of these elements into Holabird and Roche's addition constituted an architectural criticism of Root's highly unorthodox design—a correction of taste.

In Gunnar Asplund's addition to the Gothenburg Law Courts, there was an apparent struggle with the problem of a lateral extension to a bilaterally symmetrical building through a series of plans and facade studies spanning the years 1913 to 1936. Here the conjunctive or disjunctive character of each scheme was dependent primarily on the choice of architectural elements or on Asplund's choice to articulate the facade as if it were a pavilionized addition, in spite of the plan which remained an extension throughout the progression of designs. In the series of well-documented schemes for the law courts, we see Asplund's changing attitude toward the classicism of the original building in light of his growing interest in modern architecture.

In 1913, Asplund won the competition for the addition to the Gothenburg Law Courts with a scheme in which he proposed a complete rebuilding of the classical facade facing Gustaf Adolf Square in a national romantic style, thereby integrating the existing building with the addition. The scheme was not built and in 1918-19 he designed a second scheme retaining the classical facade of the original building. All of Asplund's plans added a covered courtyard space ringed by new law courts. In his 1920 project he articulated the addition as a separate entity, a classical pavilion with its own centralized entry (Fig. 6). The connecting link, which was articulated as a recess in the main facade, had no real corresponding function in plan (Fig. 7). The reading of the pavilion as a discrete detached structure linked to the original also had no correspondence to the plan in which

Fig. 6. *Gunnar Asplund, Gothenburg, Law Courts Annex, 1920 project, plan.*

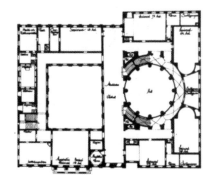

Fig. 7. *Gunnar Asplund, Gothenburg Law Courts Annex, 1920 project.*

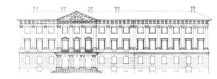

Fig. 8. *Gunnar Asplund, Gothenburg Law Courts Annex, 1934 project, elevation.*

Asplund extended the formal organization of the existing courtyard building. In his 1934 elevation study, the addition, which still replicated all the architectural elements of the original, had been integrated into a single building covered by a simple unbroken roof (Fig. 8). The facade was asymmetrical with the joint between new and old articulated by a doubled pilaster. The center of the extension was deemphasized by a solid pilaster rather than a void. In his subsequent and final designs of 1935 and 1936, Asplund changed the facade to a modern one (Fig. 9). He articulated it from the old law courts by a narrow windowless link as well as setting it back in plan. While the expressed structural grid, high base, and overall proportions of his final design can be said to sympathetically reflect the classicism of the original, Asplund never solved the problem of adding asymmetrically to a building that was already visually complete. While Asplund's addition created a second interior courtyard space and used three bays of the old facade adjacent to the porticoed entry as a shared zone of overlap in plan, this was not expressed on the new facade. Where the plan suggested that the building had been extended, the articulation of the two facades by a vertical recess introduced a different reading (Fig. 10). Yet the subtle final adjustments to the design of the facade diminished its reading as an independent structure. From the 1935 drawing to the final design of 1936, the roof overhang had been eliminated and the centered windows had been shifted asymmetrically within the articulated structural bays (Fig. 11). Along with the four fully glazed bays of the piano nobile, this clearly denied the visual center of the addition and emphasized its dependency on the original. Neither the vertical recess nor the classical bays of the original building corresponding to the zone of overlap in plan were allowed to function as a shared formal center between the two facades as indicated by the plan. The facades never attained the formal integration achieved by the elements of the plan nor did they suggest the near parity of the addition and the original structure also suggested by the plan. The four fully glazed bays of the addition with their single French balconies, like the portico of the original structure, provided a reading for the courtyard spaces behind them in plan. But because these new windows were not allowed to read as a subcenter, they could not create a new center between themselves and the classical portico. This center, which would have been in the last bay of the facade of the original structure, might have been used to visually integrate the parts. The formal relationships were so nearly solved that one can only imagine that Asplund finally chose to favor an incomplete and disjunctive reading for the

Fig. 9. *Gunnar Asplund, Gothenburg Law Courts Annex, 1934 project, elevation.*

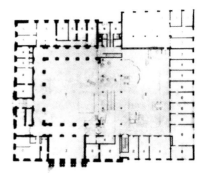

Fig. 10. *Gunnar Asplund, Gothenburg Law Courts Annex, 1934 project, plan.*

Fig. 11. *Gunnar Asplund, Gothenburg Law Courts Annex, 1934 project, final elevation as built.*

addition, emphasizing the asymmetry of the enlarged structure. This seems to be a formal choice consistent with the compositional preferences of modern architecture.

Thomas Jefferson's Monticello came to its present form through an extension which completed the already complete structure. Jefferson had begun making plans for the structure as early as 1767 based on his study of James Gibb and Palladio. The first version, finished by 1782, survives only in drawings and written descriptions and is believed to have had an entry porch with columns with a second story portico in the manner of Palladio's Villa Pisani.

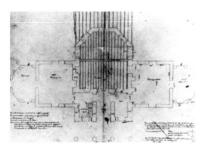

Fig. 12a. *Thomas Jefferson, plan of Montecello, first version, c. 1771.*

In 1784, Jefferson went abroad returning in 1789 when he was named Secretary of State. Upon his return, he began to plan remodeling and enlarging Monticello. Jefferson decided to add a mezzanine, skylights, and bedrooms while giving the house the appearance of a one-story building—then fashionable in France. His new plan doubled the house in width. He added a hallway along the length of the house's eastern front and in front of this he added to each side of the new entrance hall and portico, a suite of two rooms symmetrical with those of the existing structure. Where the original Monticello had been a simple linear plan of rooms symmetrical about its cross axis, Jefferson's addition was a frontal extension, completing the form of the building by introducing a new axis of symmetry perpendicular to the existing one. Except for the projecting bay of the parlor and the slightly recessed entry hall behind the east and west porticoes, Jefferson's addition completed and visually transformed the appearance of the building by establishing the bilateral symmetry of its forms about the building's two major axes (Fig. 12a, 12b).

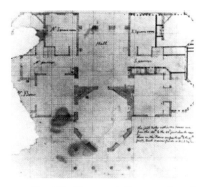

Fig. 12b. *Thomas Jefferson, plan of Montecello, final version, c. 1796.*

The Massachusetts State House was designed by Charles Bulfinch early in his career and was built atop Beacon Hill in Boston in 1795-98 (Fig. 13). A brick and wood structure with a porch of Corinthian columns and a dome, it received five conjunctive extensions between 1831 and 1917, two of which were larger than the original Bulfinch building. The first two additions extended the building to the north. The first of these was designed and built by Isaiah Rogers in 1831 and was incorporated into the second and larger addition designed by Gridley J. F. Bryant and built in 1853-56. Bryant's addition extended the materials, arched piano nobile windows, string courses, and rusticated basement of the original (Fig. 14). Among the changes that had already been made to the Bulfinch structure, prior to its expansion, were the addition of the basement, the removal of chimneys (as the heating system was modernized) and east and west entrances, and the continuation

Fig. 13. *Charles Bulfinch, Massachusetts State House. Drawing by Andrew Jackson Davis, 1828.*

Fig. 14. *Gidley J.F. Bryant, addition to tlze Massachusetts State House, 1853-56.*

Fig. 15. *Charles E. Brigham, addition to the Massachusetts State House, 1895.*

of the roof balustrade of the front porch around the entire building. The dome was originally whitewashed shingles. In 1802, it was covered with copper and later it was gold leafed. Likewise, the exterior of the Bulfinch building was painted white in 1825 and yellow in the 1850s. The extension to the north, designed by Charles E. Brigham, replaced the two earlier additions and was built of yellow brick to match the color of the state house at that time. Begun in 1889 and completed in 1895, the addition was over six times the size of the original and spanned over Mt. Vernon Street (Figs. 15, 16). As an extension, the Brigham addition formed a skillful completion of the already visually complete Bulfinch structure. It turned the original building into one of two not quite identical end pavilions. The importance of the original Bulfinch structure was retained because it continued to function as an entry front and because the new pedimented central pavilion of the addition had been made recessive by its architectural treatment and by its lack of an entrance.

Fig. 16. *Charles E. Brigham, addition to the Massachusetts State House, 1895.*

One last addition was made to the Massachusetts State House that again affected a transformation of the building. In 1917, two symmetrical wings were added to the east and west faces of the original Bulfinch structure (Fig. 17). The wings extended forward from the building, framing it and its dome. The architects, William Chapman, R. Clipson Sturgis, and Robert D. Andrews extended the rusticated basement, cornice, roof, and roof balustrades. Another floor and a row of attic windows was added within the same height as the Bulfinch structure with no attempt to match the windows or window alignment as the Brigham addition had so carefully done. The new addition was built of white marble and granite and the original brick state house was again repainted, this time white to match the marble. The two added wings, although not very skillful, do form a completion of the original structure which is given the role of a central pavilion. The Brigham addition,

Fig. 17. *Chapman, Sturgis and Andrews, addition to the Massachusetts State House, 1917.*

which was once integrated into the whole building complex, was made to function as a disjunctive addition to the rear of the new main structure. Extending back along the cross axis, it was visually isolated from the Bulfinch building which was returned to a position of primary importance.

The church of St. Maria Maggiore mentioned earlier, is an example of a concentric extension, as is the Basilica in Vicenza. For the Basilica, Andrea Palladio's first public commission, he constructed a two-story loggia around the Palazzo dell Ragione, the meeting hall of Vicenza's Council of the Four Hundred (Fig. 18). The addition successfully regularized an irregular trapezoidal plan and covered up the original building's out of fashion facade (Fig. 19). So completely was the medieval building disguised, that in Palladio's treatise, *Il Quattro Libri,* the Basilica is illustrated as an ideal project for a town hall (Fig. 20).

With concentric extensions there is the potential for a dialectic between two totally dissimilar formal systems, without the problem of a reversal of meaning between primary and secondary parts. This is due to the inherent importance of the central figure. In the most improbable of additions—Frank Gehry's house in Los Angeles—clapboard Victoriana and punk-tech converse across a space created to serve as kitchen, dining room, and sunporch (Fig. 21). Here the large scale features of the nucleus, the entryway, and bay windows of the old house are allowed to create corresponding parts in the new outer wall of the addition. The importance of the house as a central element is maintained in spite of the contrast between the two structures. While the formal order of the addition conjunctively relates to corresponding elements of the original structure, the architectural elements are totally different. Gehry's addition offers, in its contrast with the original, a critique of the architectural and social values it represents. At the simplest level, the original makes no recognition of its corner site. Where we would expect a porch or corner bay, the original house has none. Gehry's addition corrects this condition, but it is the palette of materials and details which are the real elements of the criticism. The bay window becomes a polygonal prism of glass, the clapboard is transformed into corrugated metal siding, and residential porch trellising is suggested by metal chain-link fencing. While these are visually believable as formal transformations, as industrial materials their associative meaning is not just nonresidential, it is anti-residential. They announce in a violent way that Mr. Gehry's values are not suburban values and that he shares neither the conventions nor the ideals of his neighbors.

Fig. 18. *Andrea Palladio, Basilica, Vicenza.*

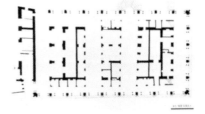

Fig. 19. *Andrea Palladio, plan of Basilica, Vicenza.*

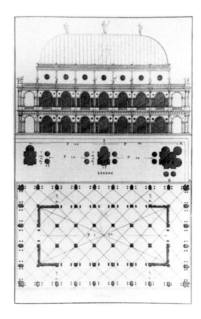

Fig. 20. *Andrea Palladio, plan of Basilica from Il Quatro Libri.*

Fig. 21. *Frank O. Gehry, Gehry House Addition. Los Angeles.*

The addition to the Boston Custom House is an example of a vertical extension which is a completion of the formal organization of the building. The original Custom House was built between 1837 and 1847 by Ammi B. Young (Fig. 22). It was a Greek revival temple with a cruciform plan originally topped by a dome. In 1913, Peabody and Stearns added a thirty-story office tower to the original structure (Fig. 23). This was supported on trusses over the existing dome. The interior was retained and new high windows at the bottom of the tower emitted light into the rotunda. While the tower is larger than the original building, it retains the hierarchy of the original formal organization. The cruciform ground plan, which was extended vertically at its crossing by a dome, is now extended by the tower whose materials and classical details also form an extension of the original building.

The addition to the Berliner Tageblatt building, a vertical extension done between 1921 and 1923 by Eric Mendelsohn and Richard Neutra, added two and one half floors to an existing five-story nineteenth century building (Fig. 24). Mendelsohn and Neutra also rebuilt all eight floors of the newspaper building's main corner above its entrance. The addition is "streamlined" in style like Mendelsohn's other expressionistic work of this period. The new addition is clearly set in contrast to the old building, no doubt announcing the newspaper's progressive self-image. In spite of the contrast of architectural elements, the effect of the addition is not disjunctive. The corner containing the entrance and a corner office for the publisher, Lachmann Mosse, is clearly the building's most important part. Its articulation by a change of architectural elements is correct and appropriate. The corner becomes a knuckle or pivot connecting the two nineteenth century wings which are clearly of secondary importance. The symmetrical additions on the upper floors step down in height from the corner, their symmetry allowing them to function conjunctively as a completion of the building's form. The building is both completed and transformed by the addition, for the lower nineteenth century structure is made to function visually as a rusticated base to the new addition. This condition further defines for us the meaning of the intended contrast between the two architectural styles.

The recent Murphy/Jahn addition to the Chicago Board of Trade building is a discrete structure which is disjunctive with respect to the original building (Fig. 25). The old Board of Trade is a 45-story skyscraper designed by Holabird and Root and built in 1929. The building, because of its unique site, provides a visual terminus to LaSalle Street. Its sophisticated massing

Fig. 22. *Ammi B. Young, Boston Custom House, 1847.*

Fig. 23. *Peabody and Sterns, addition to the Boston Custom House, 1913.*

Fig. 24. *Mendelsohn and Neutra, addition to the Berliner Tageblatt Building, 1923.*

is both a skillful transition from base to tower and a solution to its urban context.

The glass curtain walled addition reiterates the form of the original building's step-back pyramid topped tower. It is the height of the Board of Trade's intermediate base and is located behind it along its central axis. The 21-story addition contains an important new space—a new trading room—as well as a tall skylit atrium surrounded by offices.

Programmatically, the addition has a high relative importance with respect to the existing building and gives the Board of Trade a new entryway from the south. While the addition might have been developed as an extension of the lower mass of the original building, this clearly was not the intention. The addition is articulated from the existing building to express its importance, yet it remains dependent on it because of its size, location, and its reiteration of the form of the older structure.

Conceptually, the addition and its connection to the original are clear. There is no linking element between the two structures, rather the connection is made in a zone of overlap. The addition, which is wider than the original, is clad in a gridded glass curtain wall that laps the limestone walls of the existing structure, setting back in steps as it ascends. Where we have come to expect, almost as a convention, that the new all-glass building will be revealed to be an extension of the glazing system of the solid walled building from which it is extruded, Helmut Jahn has reversed this reading. The solid stone mass of the old Board of Trade slides out of the addition. This impression is further fostered by the lateral curtain walls at the sides of the addition. Here a second skin of limestone panels sheathes the grid of the glass. The glass wall slides behind it and is clearly the defining surface of the building's volume. Like the solid surfaces of the Board of Trade, it appears to have been pulled out from behind these walls. While the idea works as an exposition of the relationship of the visual components of this architecture, the execution makes a formal distinction which undermines the conceptual relationship of the parts. The new limestone curtain wall is very different from the stone curtain wall of the original. Where the stone work of the original is set in a running bond like a bearing wall, the addition reveals the nonsupporting nature of the wall by setting its vertical stone panels in a stacked bond that matches the grid of the glass. This stone surface is rendered as a thin appliqué by the way in which its top edge is arbitrarily cut away. While this treatment makes the distinction between the two stone surfaces very clear, the schematic idea, a series of related alternating stone and glass skins lapping one another, would seem to call

Fig. 25. *Murphy/Jahn addition to the Chicago Board of Trade Building.*

for their visual equation.

The addition is ostensibly postmodern, borrowing the forms of an older architecture, rendering them in new materials and details and presumably evoking the associative meaning of the latter. It is also, in its form and abstracted facades, a kind of miniature of the original structure. Therefore we should be able to ask what it tells us about the older building and what the purpose of its associative meaning is. The addition does not seem to be either a criticism or an elucidation of the original in the sense previously discussed. The repetition of the Board of Trade's forms is only a device for establishing a visual relationship between the two structures at the simplest level. The gridded curtain wall is presented as the formal equivalent of the volume-enclosing surfaces of the older structure. This is further suggested by the use of mirrored and tinted glass in adjacent vertical bands recalling the windows and piers of the original. If there is an implicit criticism, it would seem to be a modernist rejection of the Board of Trade's imitation of bearing wall construction. However, it is clear that in a completely formal sense, the relationship between glass, stone, and steel structure (as revealed at the building's base) is the real subject of the addition, the visual idea by which we may understand the relationship of both the old and the new parts to the whole. Sadly, the repetition of the form of the original building cannot be seen from Van Buren, the narrow street which the addition faces.

These examples have stressed the relationship of new construction to that which already exists because we believe this to be one of the important architectural issues of our time. We have suggested that the starting point for a building addition should be the determination of appropriate programmatic and symbolic relationships between new and old construction. Analogously, an important determinant of any building's form would be its context. We may think of all buildings as additions to their immediate surroundings, thus building additions may be thought of as paradigms for new construction. This is an important tenet of contextualism as an architectural theory. Contextualism, in its emphasis on urban space, has also made clear the hierarchy that exists between spaces and buildings. In the traditional city, one of the distinctions by which we understood the social or civic importance of a structure, was the degree to which it was freestanding or otherwise articulated from its neighbors. The parallel to this has been discussed as a characteristic of disjunctive additions. To extend this urban comparison, background buildings, or urban fabric may be thought of as having been created by a large number of conjunctive

additions, extensions to the city. If we choose to think
of the built environment as always incomplete, then we have
the choice of conceiving new buildings as completions or as
extensions of their surroundings.

In the examples given we have focused primarily on
additions which were extensions of the buildings to which they
were added. Most of these were conjunctive additions, skillful
completions of the form and the fabric of the structures they
enlarged. We have emphasized this type of addition since most
additions are dependent on and less important than the buildings
to which they are added. Such additions should always be
conjunctive no matter how great the vanity of the second architect.
We have tried to find examples of additions which were
public rather than private buildings and, in doing so, considered
a number of buildings where the additions were as
large or larger than the original building. In all of these examples,
only the tower of the Boston Custom house is more
important than the original building by virtue of its size.

We have suggested that the relationship of the added part to
the original is a primary meaning of the addition, and we have
tried to suggest that the design of an addition should not be,
apriori, either an exact and slavish replication, nor a complete
visual rejection of the existing building. The choice of addition
strategy, formal organization, and architectural elements each
have a specific meaning in relation to the original building. It is
of the meaning of these elements, singly and in relation to one
another, that we must always be cognizant when we add on to
an existing structure. Adding on has been and will continue to
be an important architectural activity, for it is the way in which
buildings will survive obsolescence of size, use, appearance,
and even symbolic meaning.

Notes

[1] Eliot, T.S. "Tradition and Individual Talent." *In The Sacred Wood: Essays on Poetry and Criticism* 50. London: Methuen & Co. Ltd, 1960.

[2] Coolidge, John. "The Villa Giulia: A Study of Central Italian Architecture." *Art Bulletin* 25, no. 3 (1943): 179.

[3] Graves, Michael. "The Swedish Connection: The Complexity of the House-Concept in Teaching Architecture." *The Journal of Architectural Education* 29, no.1 (1975): 12-13.

[4] Horace Walpole's famous house, Strawberry Hill, was built as a series of additions to a small house overlooking the Thames (from 1748 on). The house was influential in the development of picturesque architecture in England. John Summerson writes: "The deliberate irregularity of the western part of Strawberry Hill was architecturally its most important innovation ... For here is no study in asymmetrical compositions as such, but simply a whimsical pursuit of those fortuitous effects which groups of ancient buildings so often give." Summerson, John. *The Pelican History of Art and Architecture in Britain 1530-1830*. Baltimore: Penguin Books, 1969.

[5] For a discussion of building additions as criticism see Murray, F. Jeffery. "Architectural Additions as a Formal Means of Establishing and Maintaining Visual Continunity in Urban Communities." Masters diss., Ohio State University, 1981.

[6] Eliot, T. S. "The Function of Criticism." *In Selected Prose of T. S. Eliot*, edited by Frank Kermode, 69. New York: Harcourt Brace Jovanovich, 1975.

[7] Condit, Carl. *The Chicago School of Architecture*. Chicago: University of Chicago Press, 1964.

In What Style Shall We Build

In *What Style Shall We Build* was the title of an early nineteenth century treatise by Heinrich Hubsch. It began a dispute between European architects in the 1830s and 40s about the choice of architectural styles as well as the development of a style appropriate to the age. This became known as the "battle of the styles" and was an attempt to argue for the appropriateness of neo-classical, neo-gothic, and romantic vernacular styles depending on the individual project. This also led to the idea of a building's having character. Character and appropriate symbolism were argued as reasons for stylistic choices. In what style we should build additions to existing buildings could be seen as a question of appropriateness. Should an addition be built in the style of the building to which it is attached?

The United States' Secretary of the Interior's Standards for additions to Historic landmark structures offered one answer to this question. It required that any addition be immediately distinguishable from the original building, and that it be removable should there be a desire to restore the landmark building to its original condition. For most additions, this is highly unlikely because of the cost of construction of all but the smallest additions. Unless an addition is dysfunctional or an eyesore it is probably there for the life of the building. Further complicating the issue, some Landmark Commissions now consider previous additions and alterations to landmarked structures to be protected as part of a building's "historic fabric."

The Secretary of the Interiors requirement that additions to landmark buildings be differentiated from the historic structure correctly identifies the major issue. This is our understanding of the hierarchical relationship of the addition to a more important, original structure. The blanket requirement of the standards simply misunderstands the way this differentiation might be perceived when an addition causes a historic landmark to be seen as background to its addition. These standards, which date from the 1960s and were adopted in 1976, are easy to understand as a reflection of attitudes of architectural theory about additions prevalent at that time. Architects sought to differentiate new architecture from historic architectural styles in favor of either abstract geometric forms or the representation of a building's mode of construction. The result was additions that were physically separated by the nature of their connection, and were visually different in form and material from the structure onto which they were added. The meaning of such additions, intended or not, was a pejorative attitude toward existing older structures. This pejorative attitude was the same as that of the utopian social programs of the modern movement in architecture of the 1920s. Existing structures were taken to represent an outdated and undesirable social order, one representing the concentration of wealth and power among the few. New architecture represented a new social order, a better life for all brought about by modern industry. Its buildings were intended as models for rebuilding the world. This position has been somewhat tempered over the years by the failure of architecture to bring about social change and later in part by Postmodernism's re-examination of architectural history and by the re-evaluated role of compositional principles in architectural design. Some Landmark Commissions now have adopted standards for the alteration and addition to historic structures that are far more sympathetic to the idea of additions which are in the style of the existing building. Our local (Evanston, Illinois) preservation commission's standards for additions to landmark buildings now includes language such as "Innovative design for alterations to existing properties shall not be discouraged when such alterations do not destroy significant historic, cultural, architectural or archaeological material, and such design is compatible with the features, size, scale, proportion, massing, color, material and character of the property, neighborhood and environment." Setting aside the question of what constitutes innovative design, now usually interpreted as modernist, the latter part of this statement sets forth an ideal for what additions to existing historic structures should be; compatible and sympathetic with the existing building.

The history of strategies for adding to older buildings begins in the 19th century with the desire to preserve historic buildings, antique ruins, and medieval churches. This involved the repair and restoration of these structures including the acknowledgement that many of them were progressively altered over time, calling into question their original design versus the state of the inherited structure. In England, the preservation movement began with the writings of John Ruskin (1819-1900) and later William Morris (1834-1896) and the Society for the Protection of Ancient Buildings. Ruskin advocated an approach that rejected any alterations to these buildings, believing that "it is impossible, as impossible as to raise the dead, to restore anything that has ever been great or beautiful in architecture." The idea that missing portions of a building might be restored through contemporary construction was an anathema. Ruskin and Morris are the origin of the belief that any new materials added to historic structures need to be clearly differentiated from the original structure. This could be contrasted with the ideas of Eugene Emmanuel Viollet-le-Duc (1814-1879). Le-Duc was responsible for the restoration of buildings damaged during the French Revolution as well as the restoration of historic monuments. In the entry on restoration in his *Dictionnaire Raisonne de l'Architecture Francaise* he wrote, "To restore an edifice means neither to maintain it, nor to repair it, nor to rebuild it; it means to reestablish it in a finished state which may in fact never have existed at any given time." Famously Le-Duc added a gothic-style spire he designed for Notre Dame Cathedral in Paris to replace the one that had been destroyed. In the *Future of the Past,* Steven Semes writes of Le-Duc, "A superb designer, he did not hesitate to add elements to a building he thought should be present even if they had never existed historically," (Semes 2009, 119). This reminds us of the suggestion made by architect Michael Graves, that building additions could be thought of as the completion of a building imagined to be an incomplete fragment of a larger whole.

In the past, architectural theory presented reasons for making architectural and stylistic decisions. This varied from advice about the siting of buildings, the building of foundations, and the choice of architectural elements usually based on their iconography or symbolic meaning. In the first seventy-five years of the twentieth century, theory focused on functionalism and structural determinism as the starting point for architectural design. Structural determinism, or more often structural expressionism dates back to the nineteenth century's Gothic Revival and the idea that buildings should express the truth of materials. This was an expressive doctrine based on Ruskinian moralism. This would lead to the twentieth century's idea of functionalism, the idea that a building's use determined its form. In the twentieth century, the description of a building's use was not its civic, institutional, or private place in society or the city, but was described by a building's program of required spaces and the activities to be accommodated. The arrangement of these and their exterior expression became the basis of architectural design. An architectural language that was symbolic and representational was supplanted by primary geometric forms. Architectural theory, since the mid-nineteenth century, sought starting points for making architectural design choices that architects could believe in. More recently, architectural theory began to appropriate ideas and world views from nineteenth and twentieth century philosophy leading to the avant garde stance of distancing itself from both culture and society and abandoning ideas that could be directly applied to the decision-making process of architectural design. Theory no longer addressed questions of making, such as how big, how tall, or of what materials a building should be made.

In the 1970s, contextualism represented a new set of ideas that were in the air and became a part of postmodernism. Versions of these ideas appeared in the writing of various authors from Robert Venturi to Colin Rowe. Contextualism offered a theory that promoted existing conditions, the site, adjacent building fabric, and the tradition of building in a specific geographical local as a determinant of urban and architectural form. This was part of a critique of the negative impact of modernist building on existing cities. For architecture, contextualism suggested that all buildings can be seen as additions to their existing context. Where the project is an addition, the existing building would be the context. Contextualism sought to create another conceptual tool to add to those already in use by architects. Its purpose was to negate the idea that all design problems needed to be approached as a tabula rosa and put forward the idea that the built, natural, historic, and cultural environment could be a starting point in the design process.

For building additions, valuing the existing building suggests a hierarchy of importance in which the existing building is primary, and most additions are secondary. Is a building addition required by its use to be more or less important than what it is added on to? Should an addition be rendered as distinct and more important than its surroundings or should it be understood as an extension of those surroundings?

In making additions to existing buildings, the meaning conveyed by the addition, as suggested in "On Adding On," is dependent on the degree of physical and visual detachment of the addition and its relationship to the existing building. All additions to existing buildings have meaning and the source of this meaning is twofold. The iconographic and associative meaning provided by an addition's formal language and the meaning suggested by the formal relationship of the added part to the whole. Additions to existing buildings can suggest a value judgement about the importance and architectural quality of the building being enlarged and perhaps the world view it represented. This idea can be used to determine choices about configuration and architectural language to be used when we add onto an existing structure.

While these issues apply to all building additions, the relationship between the parts of a house is set by cultural norms over time. They change very slowly with changes in lifestyles, determining how we live in our houses. This establishes the relative importance of the elements of a house. Should we still design houses with separate formal dining rooms rather than informal eating spaces that are a part of a kitchen or family room? Which spaces added to a house deserve to be expressed through formal or stylistic differentiation from the existing house in terms of their importance? A library, a trophy room, an art gallery, a media center/home movie theater, a gym, or indoor swimming pool? These distinctions might dictate the appropriateness of choosing to make an addition as a distinct pavilion rather than an extension. What about materials and details? Should they reinforce the distinction or suggest integration into the architecture of the existing structure? Sometimes the relative size of an addition enters the consideration. Is it ever all right for the "tail to wag the dog?" Some additions suggest that they are unique in relation to the original building, when, in fact, the use of the spaces they contain do not support their prominence. Additions, when they are smaller in size than the original building, may become one of a series of connected parts that constitute a new, enlarged entity. When an addition is much smaller than the original and it is treated as a distinct, separate element, the form of the addition can force the original building to act as a background with the addition perceived as a foreground figure. This often reverses the perceived importance of the addition relative to the original structure. If the original is a simple volume, enlarging it by adding a new structure completely differentiated from the original may also give the addition undo importance. This can also be the result of differences in form and volumetric massing, or a change in architectural vocabulary. This would seem to suggest that the differentiation of an addition from the original building may often miscommunicate the actual importance of the addition's use.

Commercial and institutional buildings can offer examples of articulated building parts that reflect their importance such as auditoria, special collection rooms, rare book rooms, courtrooms, or other types of public meeting rooms such as council chambers; however, it would be hard to think of an equivalent in residential construction. Certainly not a kitchen, family room or principal bedroom. Most building additions are extensions of the existing building, whether these extensions are made laterally, concentrically, or vertically. Pavilions as additions are a unique case. They should be justified by the relative importance of the addition in relation to the existing structure or by the need to preserve existing features of the original building by holding the addition away.

Often residential commissions involve only the modification or reconfiguring of interior spaces. Just as additions can be thought of as extensions of the existing characteristics of a structure, architectural interiors can also be thought of as sympathetic extensions. If a building has traditional trim at window and door openings, base, and crown moldings these can be duplicated or modified for use in an addition. Modifications can include the simplification of profiles often as part of a scaling down that may be appropriate to new room sizes and ceiling heights. Special window and door head details such as crowns or pediments or simpler assemblies with parting stops, when continued into an addition, will provide a sense of continuity rather than the feeling of having stepped from one world into another. Doorways as opposed to wide openings between existing rooms and spaces that are additions can help mediate a change in the character of materials, finishes, and details between old and new. The same is true for interior doors and the selection of hardware. The choice of panelized versus flush doors, the number and configuration of panels in a door and the profile of panel stops, as well as the dimensions for stiles and rails all help to provide a sense of visual continuity between old and new. It is important to remember that just as the old structure can inform the new, in decisions made about additions, the new can inform the old. A change from five panel doors to two panels or to single panel doors or even flush doors may suggest the need to change all of the doors in a house for visual continuity where visual continuity is appropriate to the hierarchical relationship between an addition and an existing structure. Subdivisions in both doors and windows provide scale and this should be considered when changing the panel configuration of doors or the elimination of divided light windows in favor of single panes of glass. This might be called for to provide uninterrupted views, but for large areas of glass this may detract from the sense of containment provided by divided lights.

The same sorts of considerations should be given to choices about cabinetry, as most residential additions and remodeling projects involve kitchens and bathrooms. While kitchens and bathrooms have significantly changed in layout, cultural prominence, and importance over the last hundred years, cabinetry as a component is still potentially an element of continuity or discontinuity. Flush cabinet doors versus panelized, glass front versus solid panel, and full overlay doors with concealed hinges, versus stile and rail cabinetry with butt hinges are among the choices available. The choice of panel stops for paneled doors—square (shaker), ogee, oval, or custom—can be chosen or designed based on cabinetry found in the existing house. This could be cabinetry found in an existing butler's pantry, a dining or living room hutch, or even old built-in linen cabinets. These can be totally compatible with contemporary kitchen appliances, both stainless steel or appliance panels made to match the cabinetry. The introduction of foreign elements such as carved decorative corbels where details like this are not found in the existing house, or the overelaboration of cabinetry with manufactured ornament, can often make new traditional kitchens look as discordant as flush modernist cabinetry and detailing can look in an old house. Even though food was once cooked in fireplaces, exhaust hoods are not really fireplaces and may look strange when fireplace mantels are applied to them.

An exception has been in the adaptive reuse of building types that had little or nothing in the way of interior finishes and details. Light manufacturing buildings and warehouses, when repurposed, are often now designed with interior features, details, and material unrelated to the age, exterior style, or period of the building. These are most successful when they treat the original building as an enclosing shell, and new interior work is free and independent of the building enclosure, like objects in a box.

Most architects feel the need to announce their presence with their architecture. This seems to be the case whether their work is an addition to an existing building or, for that matter, an addition to a city. In his groundbreaking book, *The Design of Cities,* the late city planner Edmund Bacon put forward the idea of the "second architect," whose responsibility is to respect and enhance the quality of urban building ensembles when they are adding a new building to a significant urban space. This is a respectful attitude with implications for making additions to buildings. Old buildings are not just historical representations of their time, they are living parts of the environment that shape our emotional experiences.

Portions of the architectural profession still object to architecture that either uses traditional building forms or replicates details of existing historic buildings. In *The Architecture of Additions* (1998), one of the few books that deal exclusively with the topic, the author Paul Byard refers to building additions as "combined works" and suggests that these combined works have the ability to create new meanings. He recognizes that successful additions, "Manage the new expression so that it keeps the meaning of the old building accessible and places it in a satisfactory position in the hierarchy of the new combination." He identifies most additions as building extensions but suggests that, "The extension relies on the old as ground for its novelty." The author makes the argument that modernism and abstraction are the architecture of our time and that additions must be expressive of this idea, concluding that additions must express a difference between new and old.

For most of the architectural establishment and the self proclaimed avant garde, their rejection of new traditional architecture argues that it represents nostalgia, a longing for a less complicated past, a populist pandering to create entertainment inspired environments, or a rejection of the failed architectural experiments of Postmodernism. If we accept the directive to make an architecture of its time, then why not an architecture of its place? In the first half of the last century, modern architecture appropriated the forms of machinery to represent the technological changes the world was experiencing. In the visual arts, abstraction constituted a conscious break with the history of art as representation. But what are the forms of the technology changing the world today and how might an architecture represent the invisible digital world? What about the values of diversity and choice that contemporary democratic societies aspire to?

Can a modern abstract addition to an old building ever be sympathetic and not be perceived as demeaning? In theory, we can abstract traditional architecture into formal principles and use these as a starting point. Yet, the meaning of the new combined work—addition and original building—will always be a function of the perceived importance of the resulting parts relative to the new whole and their integration or differentiation. We create meaning through this choice. We can create a hierarchy through the location of our addition, through its size, or through its details or lack thereof.

In *S,M,L,XL,* (1995), Rem Koolhaas wrote about modernism and building size, "...all these breaks-with scale, with architectural composition, with tradition... imply the final most radical break... fuck context." This final radical break is size and Koolhaus suggests that if a building—or an addition— is big enough it becomes its own context. Rarely are additions to buildings so large that they dwarf and make irrelevant the architecture of the original building. Certainly not house additions. Further, as additions to buildings, or to our visual environment, become larger and larger, they don't often go from being foreground to being background even if they are not conceived as such.

We extend and enlarge our houses to prolong their lives and their usefulness. Making an addition is an act of appreciation and should be one of respect. Buildings can change over time in response to changes in use and circumstances. Their lives are extended through maintenance and repair, enlargement, the replacement of worn-out parts and the incorporation of new technologies. Buildings can be expanded and can contract as new uses or changes in their use require. They are susceptible to the whims of fashion and are often refreshed to align with current ideas of beauty. These changes are a natural part of a building's life cycle and should always be considered as an alternative to demolition.

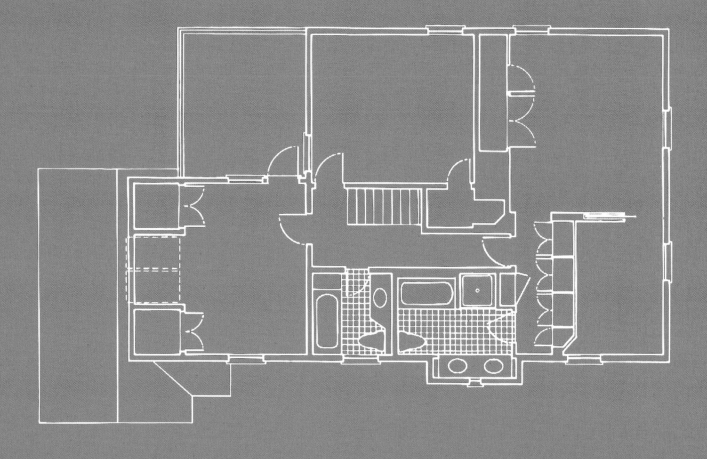

Modest Beginnings

First Additions (1974-1985)

As a small residential firm or sole practitioner, most of us began our architectural practices remodeling kitchens, bathrooms, and doing small house additions. This may vary based on location from urban to suburban to rural practices, and may vary depending on family connections and one's social circles. Over the years of our residential practice, we have done only a handful of new houses, our practice has remained primarily additions.

Early commissions are often so modest or so compromised that we later disavow them. Yet the presence of an architectural idea as a starting point in the design process should be independent of a project's size or budget. While we have been fortunate over the years to work on some wonderful old houses, early in our practice we took tiny commissions to alter builder houses from the 1950s and 60s that had no architectural merit. Most were houses that our architectural education had taught us to look down upon. We made these addition projects into an intellectual game, believing that even small additions have the power to transform houses into their better selves. We joked that while we couldn't make "a silk purse out of a sow's ear," we could make a nice pair of gloves or a belt. Choosing to begin with the form and language of an existing building raises the question of how to proceed if the building is either mundane, genuinely ill-conceived, or badly built. Additions to undistinguished buildings, unless the scope of the work includes a complete reconstruction of the original, suggested the strategy of asking which idea or architectural type the existing building was a misunderstood example of. Can we think of the new addition as an idealized version of a corrupted stylistic or architectural type?

What is the product of this attitude toward building alterations? Accepting that architectural masterworks should be, as Ruskin and Morris demanded, only restored with no changes to their appearance, leaves a world of buildings deserving of sympathetic alteration in line with Violet-le-Duc's idea that additions and restorations be thought of as enhancing and completing the original by using the existing architectural language and spatial order to make something new which incorporates the characteristics of the original.

The projects that follow illustrate the ideas contained in the essay, "On Adding On," as well as ideas about transformation. They were done between 1974 and 1985 by Stuart Cohen with his partner at the time, Anders Nereim, and Julie Hacker.

Sun Room Addition. Lateral Extension.

Done in 1974, the addition of a sunroom to the corner of a 1950s split-level ranch house was our first built commission. The addition was a lateral extension of the house's street frontage and an extrapolation of the existing forms and materials of the house, folding the window configuration of the existing house around a corner and extruding the back half of the roof to create a new sunroom space that opened to the south. The house was located on a corner, and a garden wall created a private exterior space and screened views of the street corner. We attempted to transform this ordinary 1950s split-level house by adjusting its existing forms.

Left: Before addition. **Right:** After addition with garden wall at street corner.

Home Office and 2nd Floor Bedroom Addition. Frontal and Vertical Extensions.

A more substantial addition to a two-story builder's house from the 1960s involved the addition of a doctor's office and patient waiting room for a psychiatrist who wanted to practice from home. The office included a fireplace, two walls of floor to ceiling bookcases, and a desk alcove. The addition to the front of the house was conceived as a matching piece to the house's two car garage. It was built forward to allow a new entry vestibule to separate the house from the patient's waiting area and office. The gable end of the garage was such a strong element that pairing the addition with it seemed the correct strategy despite visually equating the professional office and the garage. The skewed plan geometries of the entry way, entry hall, and waiting room, while making the movement sequence directional, date the plan stylistically to the 1970s. The addition

Left: Before addition. **Right:** After addition of new office and second-floor bedrooms.

also included the addition of two second floor bedrooms, a shared bathroom, plus the creation of a two-story stair hall. Rather than simply adding a shed dormer to create headroom for the new bedrooms, the roof was raised creating a double gable end for the main house. This transformation involved imagining that the house was part of a tradition of double gabled American and English houses.

Home office addition **Top:** Before. Plans and front elevation. **Bottom:** After addition. Plans and front elevation.

Principal Bedroom Suite and Sitting Room Addition. Frontal Extensions.

Adding to the back of a 1950s ranch style house raised the question of how it might be transformed into a version of its archetype, Frank Lloyd Wright's Usonian houses. While the work done was primarily a one-story extension across the entire rear of the house, adding a new primary bedroom suite at one side of the house, a story and a half high extension of the living and dining area, and a den-library on the other side, the scope of the work also allowed us to reside the entire house. Alternating wide and narrow width lapped bevel siding visually helped reinforce the house's horizontality and tie the existing and new parts of the house together. The new alternating width siding intentionally recalls Wright's early work, such as his 1898 River Forest Golf Club or his 1905 Glasner House.

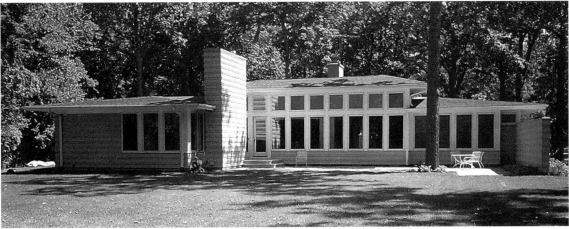

Top: Before addition. **Bottom:** After addition at the back of the house.

Screen Porch Addition. Lateral Extension.

Just as our strategy for extending undistinguished one-story mid-century ranch houses was to imagine that they could be Usonian, we tried to introduce classically correct elements to a bad builder colonial house. These were a counterpoint to the entasis-less fluted cylinders without capitals used as porch columns. Our modest addition of a one-story screened porch to this 1950s suburban house balances the one-story garage as a symmetrical element about the house's front-facing gable. The side-facing gable of the sunporch and the new matching decorative wreath suggests that the addition, despite an attempt to be more classically correct, is a miniaturization of the main house; a "mama bear-baby bear addition."

The idea of an addition as a miniature of the principal building is often a strategy seen in pavilioned structures. Levi Strauss explained our fascination with miniatures and scale models by suggesting that they have the power to reverse the way we understand the world. Allowing us to understand a thing all at once rather than working from the parts to an understanding of the whole. Here, the intent was to provide a criticism and correction of the existing architecture. This project was built but never photographed.

Top: After addition showing new screen porch to the left of the portico. **Bottom:** End elevation of screen porch.

2nd Floor Principal Suite and Bedroom Addition. Frontal and Lateral Extensions.

Enlarging the principal bathroom located at the front of a modest 1940s Colonial was an opportunity to give greater prominence to this house's entryway. It was part of a project which was to create a principal bedroom suite as well as adding additional bedrooms by building over the garage and the one-story portion of the existing house. The proposed additions would have transformed the streetfront and better integrated the existing one car garage and service entrance. This project was never built.

Left: Before addition. Existing House. **Middle:** After. New entry portico and second-floor addition.
Right: Section through entry portico and bathroom.

Kitchen and Family Room Addition. Lateral Extension, Infill.

In the mid-1970s, we were asked to add onto a stucco Mediterranean-style house located at the end of a long driveway. The house had a detached garage connected to the house by a breezeway. The garage was built perpendicular to the driveway and to a one-story bedroom wing that was also skewed to the main portion of the house. The client wanted a remodeled kitchen and a new breakfast and family room space with a direct connection to the garage. The addition had to be done to retain the raised back terrace and exterior stair to the second floor. The back of the family room facing the driveway curves and is a solid wall of bookcases. The family room would have been down several steps from the breakfast area but still open to the kitchen. The curved kitchen counter and the geometry of the kitchen functions as a knuckle to adjust the geometry of the kitchen from the grid of the house to the grid of the garage. The back edge of the family room was to be top lit by an angled skylight. This project was never built.

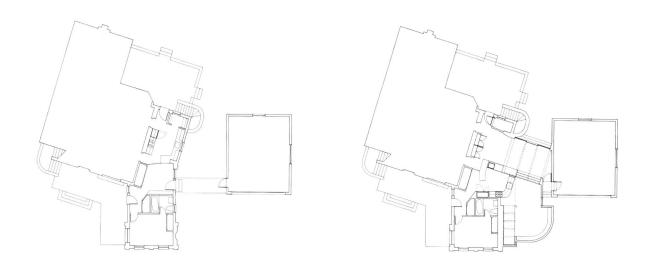

Left: Before plan. Right: After. Plan of addition.

Top Left: Before. Photo of existing house. Top Right: After. Photo of model showing addition.
Bottom Left: Before photo of front of house. Bottom Right: After photo of model showing addition.

Attached Garage, Mudroom, and 2nd floor Bedroom Addition. Lateral Extension.

Creating a lateral extension to this turn-of-the-century Arts and Crafts style house involved the replication of already existing elements and the addition of elements that had never existed as part of the original house. The addition was comprised of a new attached two car garage, a covered porch to access the back door of the house in its original location, enlargement of both the kitchen and mud room-rear entry, and on the second floor of the addition the creation of two new bedrooms and a shared bathroom. The size, shape, and leaded glass divisions of the original second floor windows were duplicated, along with a new roof dormer to match the existing one and these were arranged on vertical centers like the composition of the house's original facade.

Top Left: Before. Existing house. **Top Right:** After. Garage and bedroom addition.
Bottom Left: Detail of Decorative brackets on existing house.
Bottom Right: Detail showing cruciform column capitals based on existing brackets.

Top Left: Before. Existing end wall of house. **Top Right:** Before. Existing front elevation.
Bottom Left: After. Elevation of garage and covered arcade to existing back door. **Bottom Right:** After. Front façade.

The house above the covered porch leading to the backdoor was held up on new slightly splayed brick piers forming an arcade, a new element not found elsewhere on the house. The splay of the columns was a reiteration of the splay of the projecting brick front entryway. The brick piers were given wood cruciform-shaped capitals based on the decorative wood brackets located just below the house's second-floor overhang. This repurposing of the wood brackets as column capitols was an invention based on the language of the house.

Screen Porch Addition. Lateral Extension.

Many of our early additions, such as this screened porch added to a 1960s midcentury modern house by Chicago architect George Fred Keck, were very modest and involved simple extensions of the forms and visual language of the original structure. The new screen porch addition, located off the dining area, involved adding new windows and doors to the solid brick end wall which had denied outdoor access to much of the property previously. The first-floor living spaces opened only to a narrow side yard overlooking a wooded ravine cutting the living spaces off from direct access to the back yard.

Left: Before. **Right:** After. Screen porch addition.

Coach House

Evanston, Illinois, a suburb immediately north of Chicago, employs a system of alleys serving as garages, providing access to coach houses, and for providing for garbage pickup. Not just garages, these coach house structures had tiny second-floor apartments originally for full-time employees, often cooks or gardeners and chauffer-mechanics. The expansion of this coach house was to create a mother-in-law guest suite with the addition of garage space for two additional cars and additional parking spaces adjacent to the alley.

The existing interior stair went up to a single large room with a tiny kitchen and bath. This was expanded into a spacious one-bedroom apartment with a much larger kitchen and a full bath. The existing coach house was enlarged by an extension built in line with the existing façade facing the yard behind the main house. This face of the

Top Left: Before. Existing Coach house. Top Right: After. Coach house with addition and garden wall to screen alley parking pad from the back yard. Bottom left: Before. Alley side.
Bottom right: Addition of two car garage and expanded apartment above.

coach house was further extended by a contiguous, high garden wall screening the new alley parking apron and parking spaces from view.

The expansion used the roof forms, roof overhang details, and dormers typical of the existing coach house and of the main house, a stately stucco and timber "Prairie Tudor" structure. Built before the First World War the house and its coach house was the work of well known Chicago firm, Mayo and Mayo, who designed large houses along Chicago's fashionable North Shore.

Conclusion

These projects illustrate the ideas contained in Cohen's original essay, "On Adding On." Hopefully, they demonstrate that the choices made can transform an existing house. We believe that any opportunity to build no matter how small offers an opportunity to make "Architecture."

NEW WOOD RAKE
BOARD & TRIM

±6:12

12:12

2x4 CASING
2x SILL

RETURN ROOF
BACK. PROVIDE
FLASHING &
COUNTER
FLASHING.

4.5:12

12:12

NEW BEVEL LAP SIDING TO
MATCH EXISTING. EXPOSURE
TO ALIGN WITH MASTER
BATH DORMER.

PROVIDE METAL HEAD
FLASHING ABOVE
HEAD CASING. PAINT
TO MATCH TRIM.

03

5'-5"

ESCAPE WINDOW

NEW D.S. RUN
DOWN TO NEW
GUTTER

6
A4.0

SHIELD

NEW CEDAR ROOFING
TO MATCH EXISTING

LAP ICE
MIN. 6"
SURFAC

11

10

09

Selected Projects

(1986-2023)

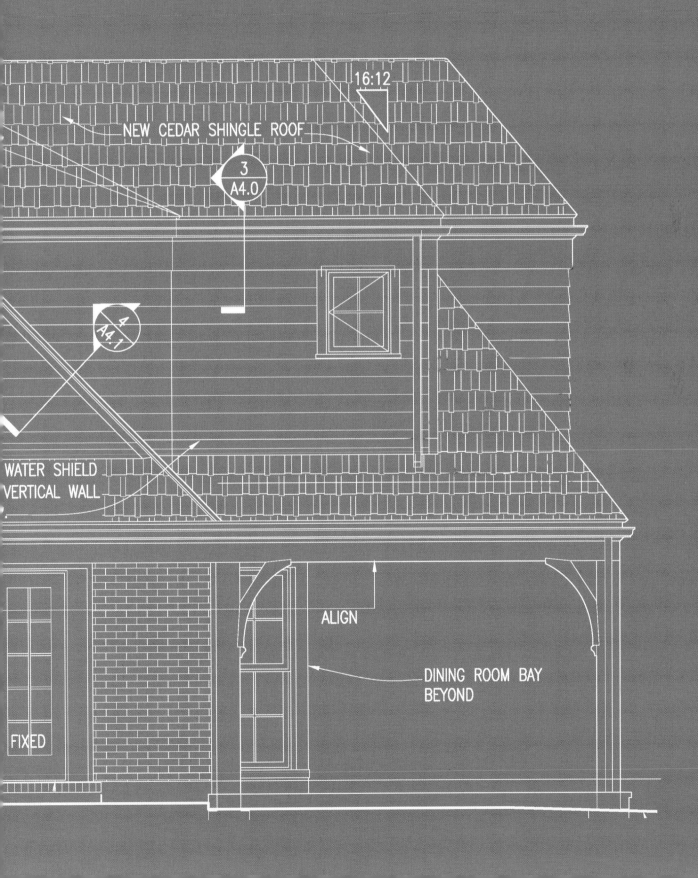

Prairie Landmark

The Kearney House was built in 1911 by Dwight Perkins and is a designated landmark. By this time, Perkins was nationally known for transforming the design of public schools during his tenure as Chief Architect for the Chicago Board of Education. He was responsible for incorporating wider interior hallways, better natural lighting, toilets on every floor of multistory schools, auditorium spaces, and playground spaces in school designs—all features public schools lacked at the beginning of the twentieth century.

Before being appointed to this position, Perkins shared office space with Frank Lloyd Wright, Myron Hunt (who would later move to California), and Robert Spencer. They worked together for four years in Steinway Hall, a high-rise office building Perkins designed in downtown Chicago in 1895. The building's primary tenant was the mid-west distributor for Steinway pianos. At the same time, Perkins lived in Evanston, Illinois, down the street from the Kearneys. Their house was one of three houses he designed within a few blocks of where he lived.

The nested gables at the front of the Kearney House are like the roof forms of Perkins' Carl Shurz High School—now a Chicago Landmark— built in 1910. The plan of the Kearney House was based on the plans of several of the houses that Spencer and Wright developed as model homes for *The Ladies Home Journal.* These were published while they all worked together in Steinway Hall. The Kearney house's plan featured a great room with a central fireplace on the backwall. This extended across the front of the house combining living and dining, which originated with Spencer's ideas for *The Ladies Home Journal* or perhaps Perkin's design of a cottage built in 1900 for a friend in Booth Bay, Maine. This room, like Spencer and Wright's designs, was extended on each end by an all-glass sunporch. At the center of the great room, the fireplace was flanked by the main stairs to one side and on the other, the butler's pantry connecting to the kitchen. Like Spencer

The Kearney House from the street.

and Wright's designs, the plan was "T" shaped with the service spaces—in this case just a kitchen— off the back and a bedroom above. This portion of the house, treated as a dependency, had a hipped roof lower than the main body of the house.

Our new addition expanded the footprint of a small sympathetic one-story addition done in the 1990s. It was removed to make space for a new kitchen, family room, and dining area addition. The new family room space was big enough for a full-size dining table opposite a new fireplace and seating group. The room opens to a raised terrace defined by low walls. The design strategy was to continue the theme of nested hipped roof elements stepping down in height from the main body of the house.

While Frank Lloyd Wright's colleagues in Steinway Hall collaborated on many of their ideas about residential design, none would utilize the architectural vocabulary that characterized Wright's work and that of the Prairie School. The Kearney House with its stucco walls and battered piers, owes more to Chicago architect's fascination with the English Arts and Craft movement—and C. F. A. Voysey—than it owes to the work of the Prairie School.

The materiality of the house, its horizontal timber banding, ganged together leaded glass casement windows, roof forms, and battered piers formed such a dominant architectural vocabulary that visually

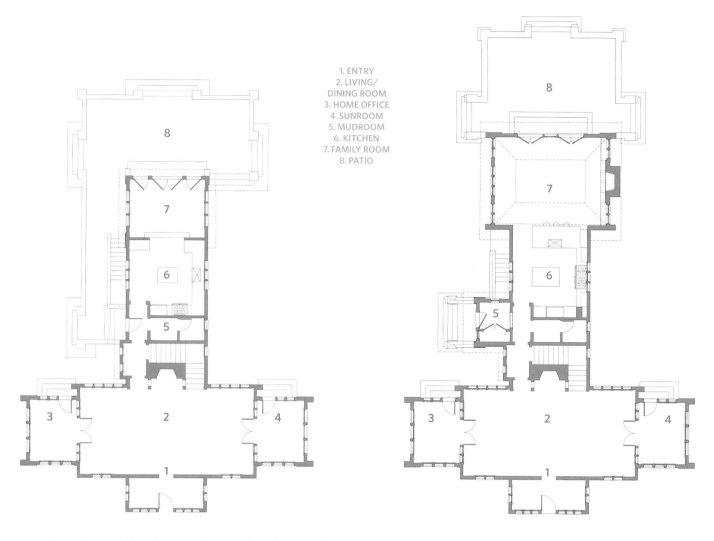

1. ENTRY
2. LIVING/ DINING ROOM
3. HOME OFFICE
4 SUNROOM
5. MUDROOM
6. KITCHEN
7. FAMILY ROOM
8. PATIO

Drawings of the Kearney House showing the first floor plans before (left) and after (right) the addition.

extending it seemed the overwhelmingly correct decision.

In the design of the new kitchen, the best layout placed the new range under the window where the original sink had been located. Ventilation for the cooktop was provided by an island-style hood that floats in front of the existing windows. These were flanked by glass-fronted cabinets visually extending the top and bottom of the windows wall to wall. A peninsula with the sink and counter seating divides the kitchen from the new great room. In this space, the fireplace is flanked by bookcases with a continuous mantel and high windows stretching the width of the room. This is a design element found in countless Arts and Crafts and Prairie style Chicago bungalows built before the First World War.

Facing east, just past the butler's pantry,

was an existing backdoor that acted as a service entry. This area was expanded into a small mudroom addition with exterior details based on the house's front sunporches. While the idea was to make the addition as seamlessly integrated into the house as possible—matching all the house's trim profiles—the owner wanted a white kitchen and white painted woodwork not the dark stained trim and cabinets of the original house.

New family room addition and new raised terrace. New side entrance and mudroom addition on the right.

The existing great room with main stair to right of the fireplace and existing butler's pantry to the left.

Above: New family room addition seen from the kitchen. Left: Kitchen peninsula from family room.

Tudor Redux

Our objective was to save this house from demolition by altering it to meet our client's needs. We tried to make these changes invisible to anyone unfamiliar with the house.

This house was built in 1913 and designed by Chicago architect Ralph Stoetzel who was noted for his Tudor Style houses, most prominently his estate house for the department store magnate William Wiebotdt. The house we added to was lived in by its second owner until 2018, when it was purchased by our client.

The exterior and principle interior features were retained and modified. The new owner wanted to keep the house's character while transforming the dark interiors into a bright, light-filled, twenty-first century home. What had been the kitchen, rear entry, back stair, attached two car garage, and low-ceilinged servant's quarters—converted into a home office by the previous owner—which extended north off the back of the house was torn down. It was replaced with a full two-story addition. This extended the footprint of the old service wing as well as the architectural character of the simple brick portions of the rear façade. The new addition contains a kitchen, breakfast area, family room, a mudroom, and a new stair down to the basement. The low-ceilinged basement was dug out by an additional four feet, completely waterproofed, and finished as additional family space and a game room. On the second floor of the addition, the upper stair hall was extended to form a furnishable area in front of the entry to the new principal bedroom suite. The secondary bedrooms and bathrooms were reconfigured, and a second-floor laundry room was added. Because the service wing had been accessed off an intermediate landing on the main stair as well as from a back service stair that was removed, the upper part of the principle stair was reconfigured and the stair was given taller, new code compliant railings and balusters. These were based on vertically extending the profiles of the

The front and rear of the house before the addition.

existing balusters, respacing them, and creating new newel posts with finials to match the existing ones. At the owners' request, the dark wood paneled entry hall and main stair were painted. New sets of French doors were added to the garden façade in the existing living room and porch. The porch was converted into a home office. All the original steel casement windows were replaced with wood thermopane windows except for the stepping windows at the main stair which had tinted glass. The wood windows were painted blue grey. On the exterior, the existing pattern of projecting brick stretchers was matched with new brick for the addition. All the brickwork was painted with masonry paint, which masked the slight color variation between the new and the old brick. A new freestanding two-car garage was attached by an arbor-covered breezeway. The interior of the house was gutted except for the paneling in the entry hall and some ceiling trim. With most of the interior plaster walls removed, new insultation, new electrical, plumbing, and new HVAC work was installed to bring the house up to today's energy standards. New interior wood millwork was made to match the profiles from the existing house.

1. ENTRY HALL
2. LIVING ROOM
3. SUN ROOM
4. DINING ROOM
5. FAMILY ROOM
6. BUTLER'S PANTRY
7. KITCHEN
8. CLOAK ROOM
9. GARAGE

1. ENTRY HALL
2. LIVING ROOM
3. STUDY 1
4. DINING ROOM
5. STUDY 2
6. BUTLER'S PANTRY
7. KITCHEN
8. BREAKFAST ROOM
9. FAMILY ROOM
10. MUDROOM
11. LOGGIA
12. GARAGE

Drawings showing the first floor plans before (top) and after (bottom) the addition.

Drawings showing the west elevation before (top) and after (bottom) the addition.

New garage with breezeway arbor connection to house.

Before (above) and after (right) pictures of the entry hall with rebuilt stairs and view into new kitchen and family room addition.

Following pages: A view from the living room through new windows in existing curving bay and new French doors.

Left: New closet and powder room from entry hall; transom windows borrow light for this interior space. Above: Looking from informal dining area into entry hall with new front door.

Left: The new kitchen, including a hidden spice rack (above) on either side of the range.

The second floor. New landing looking into the principal bedroom, which closes off with pocket doors.

Backwards House

Sometimes, additions to a house offer an opportunity to solve a fundamental flaw or to affect a change in the use of the house that has come about since it was built. This 1920 brick house is located on a large irregular property with a ravine separating it from the main street. Approached by car from the side, the formal front and main entrance to the house was built facing the heavily wooded ravine, what today would have been the principal views out from the living spaces.

The current owner had built a patio and used the space on this side of the house for informal outdoor living. The house was also accessed at the rear from a private road that serves three other houses. While this was the main approach to a house that was located at the end of the road, it also functioned as a service drive for several of the houses, including the house we altered. The private road provided access to the attached garage and facilitated deliveries to the kitchen door via a covered porch. When the main approach drive was extended to allow access to the old two-car garage, the porch at the kitchen, because of its prominence, was mistaken for the front door.

The owner wanted a mudroom entered from the garage as well as from the outside. They also wanted a new kitchen with an informal dining area that opened to their patio. The new kitchen addition also need to connect to their existing formal dining room. They also wanted a new front entrance to the house with guest closets and a connection to the main stair hall. The strategy was to wrap three sides of the existing garage, replacing a large storage shed, a garden wall, and gate. The additions to the back of the house turned it into the front entry with the addition of a new canopy covering the new front door. The old kitchen and breakfast area were converted into an entry vestibule opening to a new foyer which, in turn, connected to the house's existing stair hall. The addition that wrapped the garage provided a mudroom with an exterior entrance and connection

The original side (top) and back (bottom) of the house.

into the garage with a small office area and a built-in desk off the kitchen. At the back of the garage, the addition was treated as a pavilion to keep the roof clear of the second-floor's existing windows. The addition contains a new kitchen and a large breakfast room for informal dining. With a bay window and a high ceiling, this space overlooks the wooded ravine and opens through French doors to the existing back patio. On the exterior, we chose to match the steep roof pitch of the existing house, also matching the pattern of projecting bricks on the main house. The problem of matching the brick was simplified by the fact that the existing brick was painted. The mudroom was treated as an extruded link connecting to the volume of the kitchen and breakfast room. Inside, at the owner's suggestion, the color of the custom cabinetry was matched to photographs of the green cabinets in the kitchen of the famous chef, TV personality, and author, Julia Child.

1. ENTRY HALL
2. STAIR HALL
3. LIVING ROOM
4. SUN PORCH
5. STUDY
6. BREAKFAST ROOM
7. KITCHEN
8. DINING ROOM
9. GARAGE
10. STORAGE
11. STORAGE
12. SHED

1. ENTRY HALL
2. FOYER
3. LIBRARY
4. STAIR HALL
5. LIVING ROOM
6. SUN PORCH
7. SITTING ROOM
8. DINING ROOM
9. GARAGE
10. KITCHEN
11. BREAKFAST ROOM
12. OFFICE
13. MUDROOM

Drawings showing the first floor plans before (top) and after (middle) the addition.
Elevation of back of house (bottom) showing bay window and entry canopy at new front door.

Addition from
approach drive.

New front of house.

Left: New foyer looking into library with all new shelving and cabinetry. Above: Mudroom entry with view into office and new kitchen addition.

Breakfast area wth detail (above) of upper cabinets and spice shelf.

Prairie Jewel

This tiny one-story house is a Prairie School gem. With interconnected interior spaces and stained bands of oak trim defining the interior spaces, the rooms have an almost miniaturized quality. The house was designed by the well-known, early twentieth century Chicago architect Thomas Tallmadge (1876-1940) and his partner Vernon Watson. Tallmadge was a friend and contemporary of Frank Lloyd Wright and a longtime resident of the suburb of Evanston, Illlinois, where this house is located. In addition to being the author of several books on American architecture, Tallmadge coined the term "Chicago School" to describe the architects who were building the steel framed commercial office buildings that Chicago would become famous for. More locally, he was the designer of Evanston's streetlamps.

In addition to remodeling the kitchen, expanding it to create a breakfast bar, adding a powder room off the entry hall, and remodeling the secondary bathroom, the owner wanted to add a guest bedroom suite with a full bathroom. The addition was connected to the house by the creation of a mudroom side-entry acting as a link adjacent to the existing sunporch. This was a space with interior exposed brick walls that we painted and trimmed to match the house. The red quarry tile floor was replaced with new tile and the windows were restored and reglazed, incorporating new colored glass accents. A hallway leading from the butler's pantry to the sunporch was added and the entry to each of the existing two bedrooms was reconfigured. The addition was shifted toward the existing freestanding garage to allow an existing concrete stair down to the basement to be retained. The addition forms the back of a new courtyard space created in conjunction with the existing garage.

On the interior the existing stained oak trim and simple molding profiles, which give the house much of its character, were extended throughout the new and reconfigured spaces. The space of the tiny kitchen was visually expanded by the use of two-sided glass upper cabinets above a peninsula. The new palette of materials and colors were based on the oak woodwork and cabinetry. This was carried throughout the new work but with a slightly more contemporary sensibility.

1. ENTRY
2. KITCHEN
3. BEDROOM 1
4. BEDROOM 2
5. SUNROOM
6. DINING ROOM
7. LIVING ROOM
8. GARAGE

1. ENTRY
2. BEDROOM 1
3. SUNROOM
4. BEDROOM 2
5. BEDROOM 3
6. KITCHEN
7. DINING ROOM
8. LIVING ROOM
9. GARAGE

Plan drawings showing before (top) and after (bottom) the addition.

Elevation drawings showing before (top) and after (bottom) the addition.
Following pages: Existing living room and inglenook.

Left: New kitchen looking toward living room. Above: The kitchen looking from breakfast bar into work area.

Sun porch and new back entrance. Windows were reglazed with colored glass. Wood ceiling and floor tile are new, as is bench under windows.

Above: New bathroom in guest suite addition. Right: Remodeled hall bathroom.

Room with a View

A modest size brick house with a steep, slate covered roof and a French country ambience; this house had an awkward shed roofed one-story kitchen addition and breakfast room added on the back in the 1980s. The addition was torn down to its foundation and replaced with a new two-story addition, which was extended across the entire back of the house. The new kitchen included a two-story high breakfast area, top lit by a dormer window with scrolled wing walls detailed to match existing dormers at the front and side of the existing house. The ground floor also included a new family room with a fireplace flanked by pairs of French doors opening to the back yard. The second floor was a principal bedroom suite with the bedroom featuring a one- and one-half story tall ceiling extending into the new hipped roof. Cut into the inward sloping interior surface of the roof is an *oeil-de boeuf* dormer window top lighting the bedroom. A new walk-in closet and bathroom were located over the kitchen.

The house is on a suburban site with an ample backyard but had no views from the kitchen to the side where the adjacent house was only eight feet away. The addition was completed in 1999, and a decade later the owner was able to buy the adjacent house, which was located on a large corner lot. They decided to tear it down to create a large garden. We were asked to redesign the kitchen that we had done earlier to provide views to their new garden as well as to their existing back yard. The challenge was to design a kitchen with ample storage, counter space, and a lot of windows located where cabinets and the range hood would normally have taken up space on the exterior walls. A transition space between the kitchen and the family room was redesigned as a breakfast area allowing us to create a longer kitchen island. The sink was relocated to the new island and the range was located along an outside wall with windows behind it coming down to the counter. The owner claimed they never fried food so we didn't worry about grease splashing on the windows. To ventilate the cooktop we used a pendant "island" hood that floats in front of the new windows. These windows look out to the garden at the side of the house with a view of a small fountain. Facing the backyard, we created a wall of windows with two sided glass display cabinets in front of them. The muntin divisions in the cabinets were designed to exactly align with those in the windows behind. Because of the high ceiling at this end of the kitchen, a feature of the older kitchen we had designed, these cabinets couldn't be supported from above. They are supported by concealed steel angles mounted vertically to structural posts between the windows. With these modifications and all new cabinetry, the previous addition was transformed into a "room with a view" of their gardens.

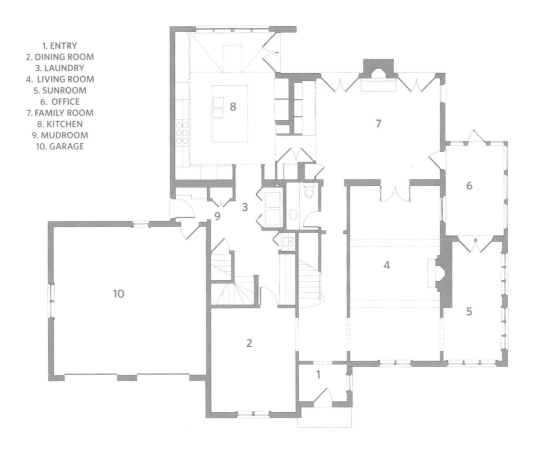

1. ENTRY
2. DINING ROOM
3. LAUNDRY
4. LIVING ROOM
5. SUNROOM
6. OFFICE
7. FAMILY ROOM
8. KITCHEN
9. MUDROOM
10. GARAGE

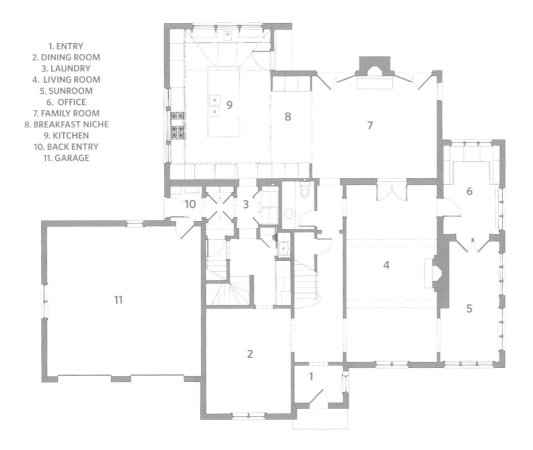

1. ENTRY
2. DINING ROOM
3. LAUNDRY
4. LIVING ROOM
5. SUNROOM
6. OFFICE
7. FAMILY ROOM
8. BREAKFAST NICHE
9. KITCHEN
10. BACK ENTRY
11. GARAGE

First floor plans before (top) showing our late 1990s kitchen and family room addition and remodeling with the principal suite above and after (bottom) the 2008 remodeling.

Overall view of kitchen with window to the backyard.

View to new side yard garden where neighboring house was located.

Breakfast area
open to kitchen and
family room.

Above: Principal bedroom with *oeil-de-boeuf* window. Right: Office off right of bedroom with pocketing French doors and a wall of storage cabinets and credenza.

French Country Reimagined

Designed by Chicago architect Robert Work, this French country style estate is characterized by its dormers, second floor bay windows, ground floor arched windows, and spire shaped peaked roofs. Robert Work had a distinguished architectural lineage. He was Howard van Doren Shaw's first employee and worked for him during the period when Shaw became one of this country's best known residential architects. He worked for Shaw until Shaw's premature death in 1926, at which time he went to work for another former Shaw employee, David Adler who became a nationally prominent classical architect.

The house sits on almost three acres of land across the street from Lake Michigan, one of the larger undivided parcels of land along Chicago's Northshore. The house had been altered over the years. The ground floor of what had been the servants' wing with its low ceilings had been converted into a large contemporary kitchen in the 1980s, with white laminate cabinets and stainless steel appliances. Above it the original servants' quarters, still intact, were tucked into the space below a sloping roof. This entire wing of the house was torn down and replaced by a large addition facing the backyard. Our addition extended the main ridge line of the house to create space with the same ceiling height as the second floor of the main house. At the other end of the house, an original one-story screened porch had received a second-story flat roofed addition in the 1990s. It contained the principal bedroom and bathroom suite. Lavish in its day with wall-to-wall marble tile, it featured a large platformed whirlpool bathtub. This portion of the second floor, including the space over the porch, was converted into two secondary bedrooms and a shared bathroom. The addition that replaced the servants' wing contained on its first floor a mudroom, half bath, kitchen, and combined informal dining and family room area. The second floor contained a laundry room, the primary

The view from the street.

bedroom, bathroom, walk-in closets and dressing area, and a covered roof terrace off the sleeping area overlooking the yard.

The strategy for the addition was to make it a lateral extension of the main house, extending the simple roof form, the materials, and architectural features of the house. The faceted, bay shaped screen porch at the south end of the house was mirrored by a bay off the family room and the covered porch above, which were part of the new addition. This bay was given a peaked roof and a new peaked roof was added over the flat roofed second floor of the existing screen porch at the other end of the house. This roof addition as an alteration to the existing house created a paired element to "bookend" the long back façade, helping to visually integrate the addition into the existing structure. Compositionally, these elements are symmetrical about the arched head French doors at the end of the entry hall. These doors center on the entry space, which is marked at the front of the house by a loggia and tall peak roofed entry pavilion. On the back façade, the flat sections continue to be visually organized by the local symmetrical arrangement of windows and second floor bays.

At the owner's request, the simple "French Country" detailing of the existing house's interior was upscaled with more elaborate classical elements.

Right: Reconfigured north addition.

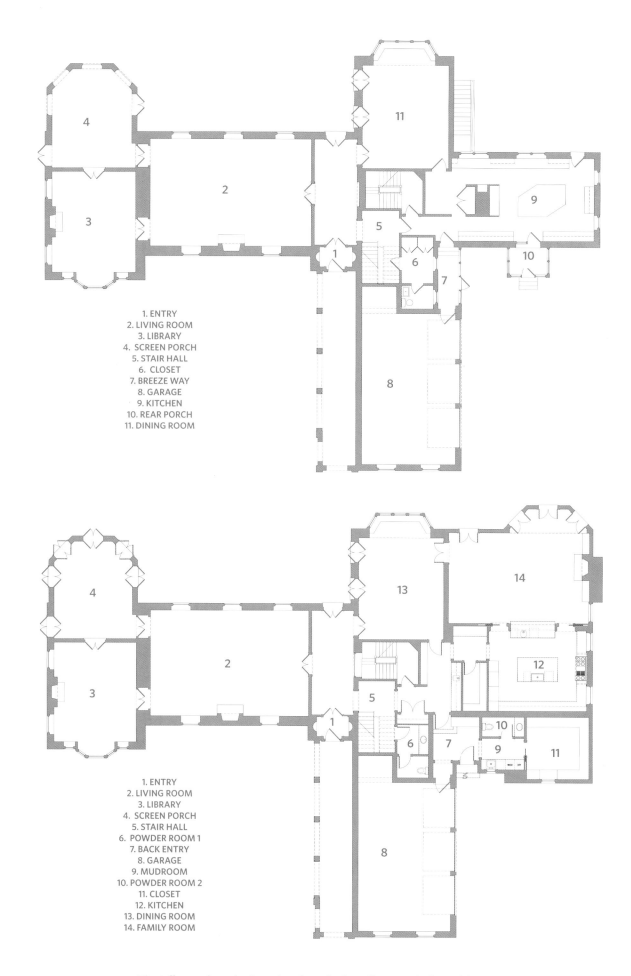

1. ENTRY
2. LIVING ROOM
3. LIBRARY
4. SCREEN PORCH
5. STAIR HALL
6. CLOSET
7. BREEZE WAY
8. GARAGE
9. KITCHEN
10. REAR PORCH
11. DINING ROOM

1. ENTRY
2. LIVING ROOM
3. LIBRARY
4. SCREEN PORCH
5. STAIR HALL
6. POWDER ROOM 1
7. BACK ENTRY
8. GARAGE
9. MUDROOM
10. POWDER ROOM 2
11. CLOSET
12. KITCHEN
13. DINING ROOM
14. FAMILY ROOM

First floor plans before (top) and after (bottom) the addition.

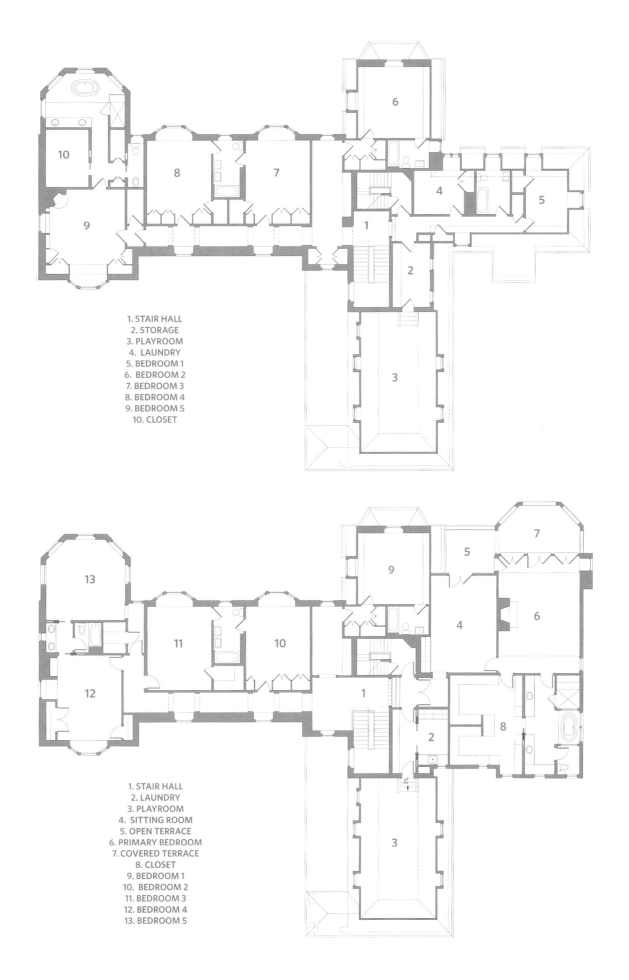

1. STAIR HALL
2. STORAGE
3. PLAYROOM
4. LAUNDRY
5. BEDROOM 1
6. BEDROOM 2
7. BEDROOM 3
8. BEDROOM 4
9. BEDROOM 5
10. CLOSET

1. STAIR HALL
2. LAUNDRY
3. PLAYROOM
4. SITTING ROOM
5. OPEN TERRACE
6. PRIMARY BEDROOM
7. COVERED TERRACE
8. CLOSET
9. BEDROOM 1
10. BEDROOM 2
11. BEDROOM 3
12. BEDROOM 4
13. BEDROOM 5

Second floor plans before (top) and after (bottom) the addition.

Top: Existing entry front. Bottom: New entry front with addition on right.

Top: Original elevation with service wing on left. Bottom: Garden elevation with addition.

North elevation drawings showing before (top) and after (bottom) the addition.

View from the
family room into the
new kitchen.

The new kitchen.

The new primary
bedroom with
French doors to
covered terrace.

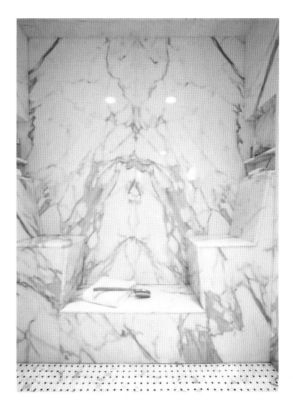

Left: Bathroom. Top: Shower and steam room. Below: Tub alcove.

133

Eclectic Country House

The design of an addition to contain a new bathroom as part of the owner's suite required a tiny extension of the existing one-story house. The back of the house curved into a horseshoe shape to create a defined terraced space. The terrace was extended and a new recessed hot tub was located steps away from the French door leading out from the new bathroom. The tiny extension was carefully detailed to reiterate the existing house and the treatment of windows and doors as shallow bays that project out to the edge of the soffit at the roof overhangs. While only one story, the house, which was built in the 1950s, is anything but a 50s ranch house. Designed by architect Robert Arnold, it was built with nine-foot ceilings, over scaled classical moldings and wainscoting, features which established the unusual character of this house. In addition to adding space for the new bathroom, the project involved the remodeling and reconfiguration of the existing owner's suite and connecting it to an adjacent bedroom to be used as an office and studio.

The existing bathrooms in the house had walls of one-inch square Bisazza-colored glass tiles from Italy. The tile color was still being manufactured, and we decided to make it a feature in the new bathroom. The center section of the bathroom has a double vanity and freestanding tub. This space is topped by a vaulted ceiling that was silver-leafed to provide a shimmering glow and match the warmth of the pewter finish on the tub. Because the shower and toilet room were against outside walls, the challenge was to light the interior spaces. The interior window over the tub corresponds to a high window opposite it in the toilet room. This also borrows natural light for the shower stall through a glass panel the full width of the space. This interior window is on the plumbing wall above a cabinet behind the toilet. All the trim and crown moldings used in the addition and remodeled spaces match the robust shapes found throughout the

Addition with French door from bathroom to terrace.

house.

The owners are art collectors. One is an interior designer who was responsible for the wonderfully eclectic quality of their furnishings.

Over the years, we've come back to help first with a remodeling of their kitchen and later with the remodeling of the two secondary bathrooms. In these, the owner wanted to replace the tubs and shower stalls and to use a larger and simpler tile. Now, the original glass Bisazza tile remains only in the house's powder room.

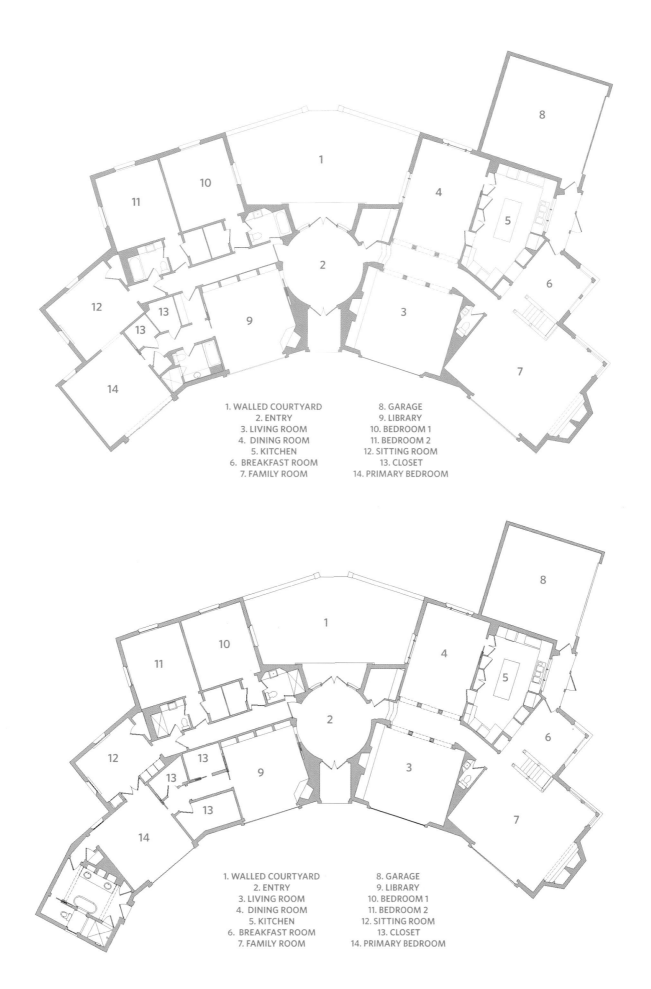

1. WALLED COURTYARD
2. ENTRY
3. LIVING ROOM
4. DINING ROOM
5. KITCHEN
6. BREAKFAST ROOM
7. FAMILY ROOM
8. GARAGE
9. LIBRARY
10. BEDROOM 1
11. BEDROOM 2
12. SITTING ROOM
13. CLOSET
14. PRIMARY BEDROOM

1. WALLED COURTYARD
2. ENTRY
3. LIVING ROOM
4. DINING ROOM
5. KITCHEN
6. BREAKFAST ROOM
7. FAMILY ROOM
8. GARAGE
9. LIBRARY
10. BEDROOM 1
11. BEDROOM 2
12. SITTING ROOM
13. CLOSET
14. PRIMARY BEDROOM

Plans before (top) and after (bottom) the addition.

Left: Vanity area looking out to terrace. Above: Bathroom with interior window and silver-leafed vaulted ceiling over tub and vanity. Following pages: Principal bedroom with door to bathroom addition on the right.

Office, formerly a
bedroom, open to
principal bedroom.

Left: Kitchen, partially remodeled. Above: Hall bathroom. New cabinetry, plumbing fittings, and stone. Shower replaces a tub-shower combination.

English Country
House Revisited

Built in the 1920s, this painted brick English-style country house was designed by Ernest Grunsfeld Jr., the architect of Chicago's Shedd Aquarium. Grunsfeld graduated from MIT, America's first school of architecture in 1919, and then attended the Ecole des Beaux Arts in Paris and the American Academy in Rome. Sited at the edge of a wooded ravine, the main body of the house opens to a south facing lawn. Extending north from the corner of the house, along the edge of the ravine, was a two-story wood sided service wing with a kitchen and butler's pantry on the first floor and a back stair accessing bedrooms above.

An old photo of this portion of the house shows a free standing, two-car garage with a tall, hipped roof immediately to the north, probably built in the 1950s. At this time, the kitchen was remodeled with a breakfast area overlooking the ravine. The kitchen was typical for its day with flush overlay doors of white plastic laminate, white plastic laminate countertops, and four inch by four inch white ceramic tile backsplashes. In the 1990s, a two-car brick garage, side entrance, and mudroom were added where the wood garage stood. The garage addition was a handsome, compatible design done in painted brick by Chicago architect Kathryn Quinn. Our first instinct was to try and save it. Because of the amount of space required for a new kitchen, breakfast room, family room, and mudroom, and the new zoning setbacks required from the edge of the ravine, the garage needed to move forward to the west on the site. A version of Quinn's garage design was reconstructed, and the service wing was extended with a higher roof ridge to match the main body of the house. This infill addition was given a new cross-gable and recessed entry to mark the house's reconfigured service entrance.

Inside the house, all the ground floor woodwork still had its original finish, and the cabinetry in the living room and the library were the starting point for integrating

New family room addition looking toward kitchen.

the new trim and cabinetry in the addition which contained the new kitchen, butler's pantry, breakfast room, family room, and new back stair. A unique feature of the cabinetry in the original house was raised diamond panels. These were matched for the upper row of kitchen cabinets which carry up to the ceiling. The kitchen cabinets were visually supported on wrought iron decorative brackets with scrolled ends.

The new back stairs arrive at a landing with very tall windows overlooking the ravine. The transom windows over the casements used in the family room continue across the wall at the side of the new back stairs. On the second floor, the stairs arrive at a new sitting area for two new children's bedrooms. Above the kitchen, space was added to the main bedroom at the corner of the existing house. This was used for walk-in-closets, a dressing area, and a new principal bathroom with a vaulted ceiling overlooking the ravine.

By pulling the garage forward, it now forms one side of an entry courtyard.

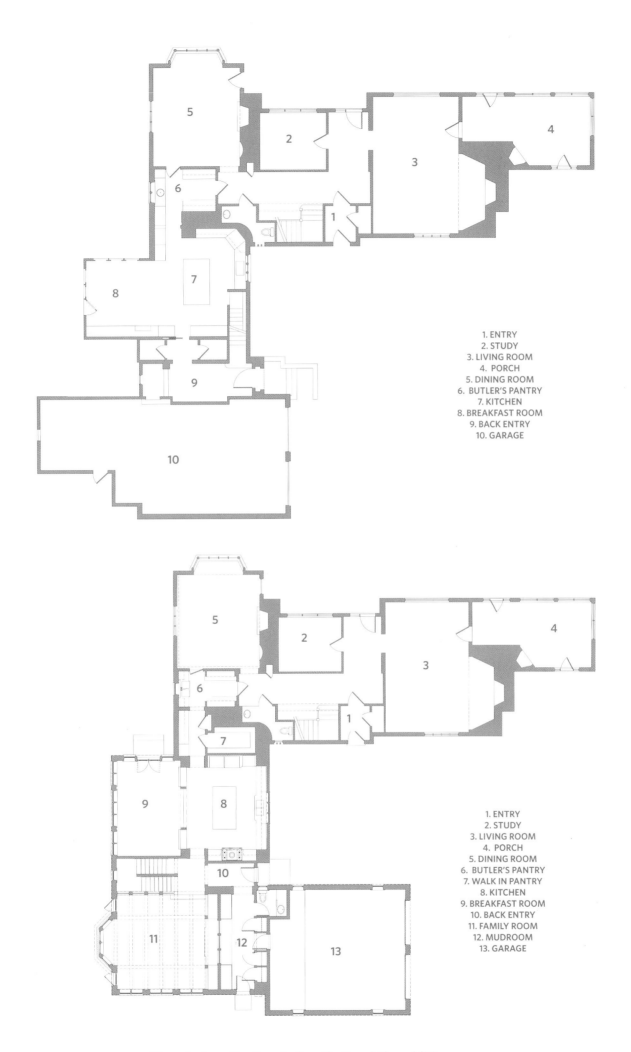

Top plan legend:

1. ENTRY
2. STUDY
3. LIVING ROOM
4. PORCH
5. DINING ROOM
6. BUTLER'S PANTRY
7. KITCHEN
8. BREAKFAST ROOM
9. BACK ENTRY
10. GARAGE

Bottom plan legend:

1. ENTRY
2. STUDY
3. LIVING ROOM
4. PORCH
5. DINING ROOM
6. BUTLER'S PANTRY
7. WALK IN PANTRY
8. KITCHEN
9. BREAKFAST ROOM
10. BACK ENTRY
11. FAMILY ROOM
12. MUDROOM
13. GARAGE

Plans before (top) and after (bottom) the addition.

Left: Kitchen range, range hood, and wrought iron brackets under cabinets. Above: Butler's Pantry.
Following pages: Breakfast area looking into kitchen with two-sided glass front display cabinet either side of doorway.

The principal bathroom. Above: Bathroom looking at shower. Translucent French door and high window light the toilet room. Right: The tub with a view of the ravine.

Banker Tudor

"Banker Tudor" was a term used for mid-sized suburban houses, nicely built with perhaps the pretention of being larger and more extravagant than they were. Built in the early 1920s, this handsome stone Tudor style house had a small, outdated kitchen and no informal family living areas. A narrow porch off the dining room and the living room had been enclosed, furnished with a sofa and a desk, and served as both a TV room and home office. We remodeled this room with the addition of French doors to provide better access to the existing raised terrace overlooking the rear yard.

The addition at the back of the house against the rear wall of the garage created a new family room adjacent to the kitchen. The kitchen, which was expanded to the west, required a flat roof over the breakfast area to allow the second-floor windows of the children's bedrooms to remain. These windows were replaced, and the sill was raised. The new family room was built down two steps from the breakfast area, placing it at grade. It was designed as a two-story space and was top lit by roof dormers and high windows along its north side, where views would have been the side wall of an adjacent house. While the entire back of the existing house was predominantly stone, the north and west sides were stucco and half timbers on the second floor above the garage. This was a portion of the house that had been bedrooms for household staff. Facing the yard, the new family room has a square bay window with a metal roof that duplicates the bay window at the west end of the dining room. The project also included the addition of a new powder room off the back hall and entry from the garage.

The north face of the family room addition was done in stucco with half timbering to relate to the adjacent garage façade. The rest of the addition was done in stone. Matching the stone proved to be a challenge. Over the years the stone, which was originally grey, had weathered to a warm, buff color. The same stone was available but when new looked distressingly different. A decision was made to look for stone that would better match the weathered color. This involved sourcing stone from several different quarries.

A few years after the kitchen and family room were completed, the same owner asked that we remodel and enlarge the principal bedroom suite. The existing principal bedroom opened onto a second-floor roof terrace with a stone parapet. The new bedroom was expanded by an addition that enclosed this space. The addition matched the adjacent gable end of the existing house. Because of the difficulty we had sourcing the stone for the first addition, we decided to make the gable end in stucco and half timbers using the north facing end of the garage as our model. The space under this roof was incorporated to create a high ceiling in the new bedroom.

The original primary bedroom had a fireplace, and this space was turned into a sitting room for the bedroom suite. As part of the addition and remodeling, a new walk-in closet and compartmented bathroom were created in the existing space.

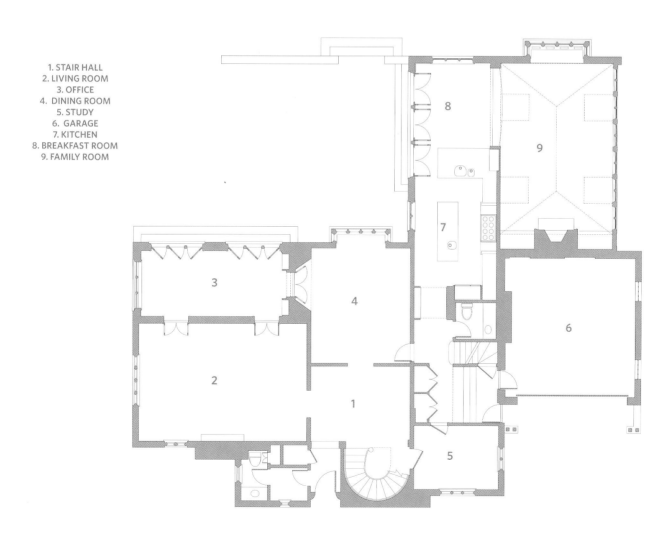

159

1. STAIR HALL
2. LIVING ROOM
3. OFFICE
4. DINING ROOM
5. STUDY
6. KITCHEN
7. GARAGE

1. STAIR HALL
2. LIVING ROOM
3. OFFICE
4. DINING ROOM
5. STUDY
6. GARAGE
7. KITCHEN
8. BREAKFAST ROOM
9. FAMILY ROOM

Plans before (top) and after (bottom) the addition.

Top: **Before.** Bottom: **After additions.**

Top: **Before.** Bottom: **After additions showing half timber side of new family room.**

Left: New family room addition. Above: Remodeled and extended kitchen.

Left: Principal bedroom addition. Above: Principal bathroom.

All Decked Out

Like many of our projects, we did work on this house over several years. A Victorian, which was stuccoed over rather than resided, the house sits on a sloping lot. A driveway on the east side of the house led to a detached two car garage in the rear yard. The change in grade cut the house off from access to outside space from the first floor rooms. The first addition to the house was a large outside deck to provide accessible space off the entire east side of the house. The sill of the windows in the front sunporch provided the starting point for the height of the stuccoed guard rail of the deck. This space, along with the existing east facing dining room, were given new French doors to the outside. Stairs down from the deck descend to both the north and the south and provided the opportunity to create a built-in bench with an open back based on the design of the famous Lutyen's garden bench.

Several years later, we were asked to add an attached garage and mudroom to the house extending the space of the existing kitchen. The kitchen and butler's pantry were reconfigured to open to the bay that became the new breakfast room with new doors to the deck.

Below: **Before and after plans for the first floor.**

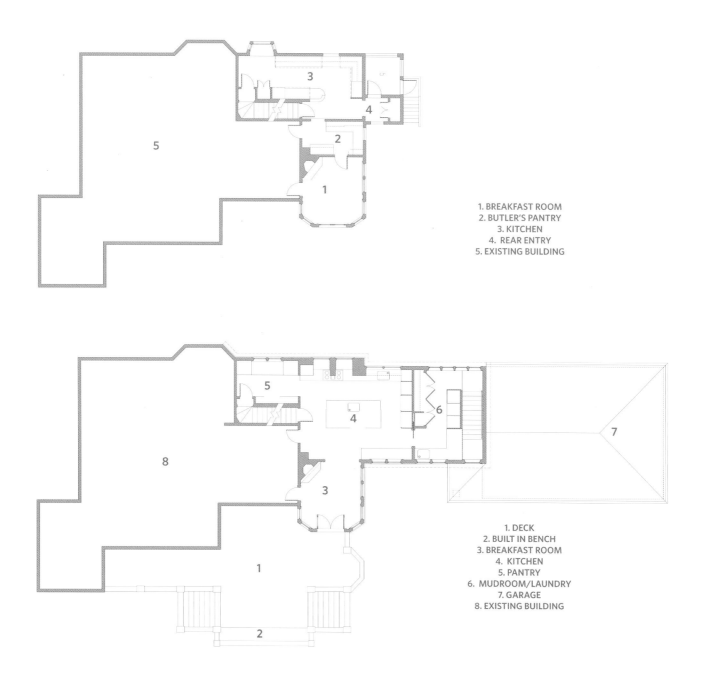

1. BREAKFAST ROOM
2. BUTLER'S PANTRY
3. KITCHEN
4. REAR ENTRY
5. EXISTING BUILDING

1. DECK
2. BUILT IN BENCH
3. BREAKFAST ROOM
4. KITCHEN
5. PANTRY
6. MUDROOM/LAUNDRY
7. GARAGE
8. EXISTING BUILDING

The new deck.

The new kitchen
with door to laundry
room and stair down
to back door and
garage at right.

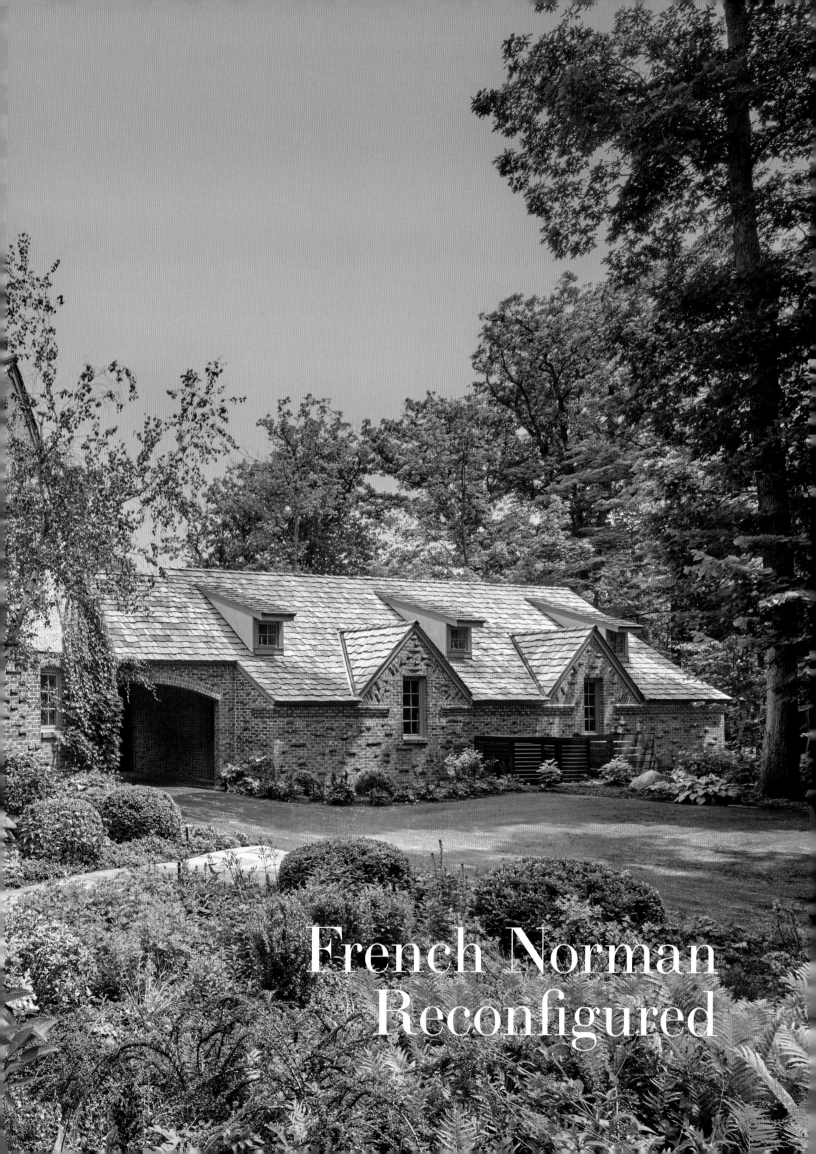

French Norman
Reconfigured

Built in the 1980s on a private road, once part of a David Adler designed estate, this house had pretensions of being a French Norman country house. Sadly, it was built with eight foot ceilings and no interesting interior features. The house was nicely sited with its back facing a heavily wooded ravine overlooked by the original kitchen with a bay window but no access to the outside. The house's expansion extended the kitchen into a new breakfast room with a new bedroom and remodeled bathroom above. All of the interior spaces were remodeled. The only change to the front of the house was the addition of a third-floor inset dormer used to top light the second-floor stair landing. New finishes were provided throughout including moldings and new cabinetry. The exterior forms were extended with the bulk of the addition at right angles to the back of the existing main house. The roof and large shed dormer at the back of the original house were turned to form the new roof, and the corner masonry columns of the existing screen porch were duplicated at the end of the new addition forming a covered porch off the new breakfast room.

On the second floor, along with the new bedroom and bathroom in the addition, the principal bedroom was reconfigured. A new principal bathroom was created in what had previously been a walk-in closet with sloping ceilings and areas of low headroom. Over the first floor screen porch, a previously unfinished space was turned into a small sitting room opening to the bedroom with a built-in desk and new dormer window.

When our original client sold the house, the next owner asked us to do an addition enlarging the garage. The existing two-car garage, which was set at an angle to the main house and connected by a covered breezeway sheltering the back door was doubled in size and expanded to house two more cars. Its low front-facing gable was replicated and parred to form a new visual center for the long façade. Since almost every inch of the existing basement was finished for use as

Top: **Original entry hall.** Bottom: **Original family room.**

a family room and game room, the garage extension provided a large, finished attic storage space. This was lit by new square windowed shed dormers that matched the new dormer we had previously added to the space over the existing screen porch. These helped to create vertical accents that mitigate the new length of the garage. For the garage addition, decorative brick corbels at the roof's eaves were carefully matched, seamlessly integrating all the additions and modifications which were done in the style of the existing house.

1. ENTRY
2. LIVING ROOM
3. PATIO
4. DINING ROOM
5. KITCHEN
6. OFFICE
7. MUDROOM
8. LAUNDRY
9. FAMILY ROOM
10. SCREENED PORCH
11. GARAGE

1. ENTRY
2. LIVING ROOM
3. PATIO
4. DINING ROOM
5. KITCHEN
6. BREAKFAST ROOM
7. OFFICE
8. MUDROOM
9. LAUNDRY
10. FAMILY ROOM
11. SCREENED PORCH
12. GARAGE

Plans before (top) and after (bottom) the addition.

Left: Back of house facing pool. Addition is on the right.   Above: Expanded garage with attic storage above. Space above screened porch was connected to the principal bedroom suite.

Left: **Entry hall after remodeling.** Right: **Remodeled stair with new balusters and railing, as seen from entry to living room.**

Left: New kitchen with knotty pine cabinets and copper hood. The form of the arched hood relates to the fireplace in the adjacent family room. Above: Kitchen looking into addition and new informal dining area with view into the wooded ravine.

Family room fireplace
with copper hood
and adjacent
new knotty pine
cabinetry. Fireplace
masonry is original.

Above: New dormer top lighting landing at top of stair.
Right: Principal bedroom with new fireplace and connection to sitting room at left.

Left: New sitting area for principal bedroom over the existing screened porch. **Above:** Closet and dressing area.

Principal bathroom formerly
closet and attic space.

Colonial Infill

Previous additions and alterations to this mid-century colonial rendered this house dysfunctional. There was no connection between the remodeled kitchen and the family room, an addition made off the back perpendicular to the house. All of the living spaces had only limited access to the rear yard and the overly large breakfast room faced the front of the house. An existing small one-car garage had been expanded forward of the house and to the north to create a large two car garage. The decision to keep the corner pier supporting the house above the existing garage rendered one of the two spaces unusable except for a subcompact car.

The one-story family room added to the back of the house terminated the space of the entry hall. It had a flat roof and parapet that was the view out the large window at the mid-landing of the main stair. This space was extended vertically into a two story high living space, and the gable roof was treated as a pavilion to avoid blocking the west light that came through the original windows at the intermediate stair landing. A dormer window at the back of the family room provided a view into the top of the room through the windows at the stair landing.

A one-story addition was stretched across the back of the house from the edge of the existing garage to the existing family room addition. This contained a new mudroom and laundry room and a new ground floor half bath. The large new kitchen opens to a large breakfast area that connects to the reconfigured terrace at the back of the house through pairs of French doors. At the south, end this space opens to the slightly reconfigured family room. A beam supports the back wall of the house above the addition. This is supported on two square columns that define the space of the kitchen from the dining area.

A second floor was added over the one-story garage, adding a full bedroom

Street view (top) and back (bottom) of the house before addition.

and bathroom to the house. The tiny bedroom that was at the back corner was converted into a laundry room, and the second floor along the front of the house was reconfigured internally to create a new principal bedroom suite.

The thematic idea of the existing house was an articulated main block with flanking wings. This established the formal language of the additions to both the front and the back of the house.

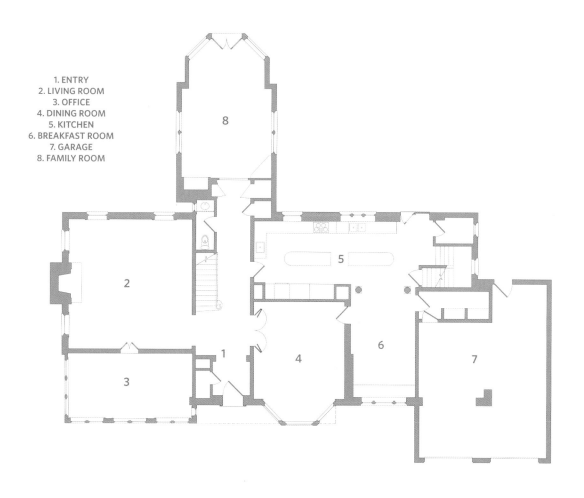

1. ENTRY
2. LIVING ROOM
3. OFFICE
4. DINING ROOM
5. KITCHEN
6. BREAKFAST ROOM
7. GARAGE
8. FAMILY ROOM

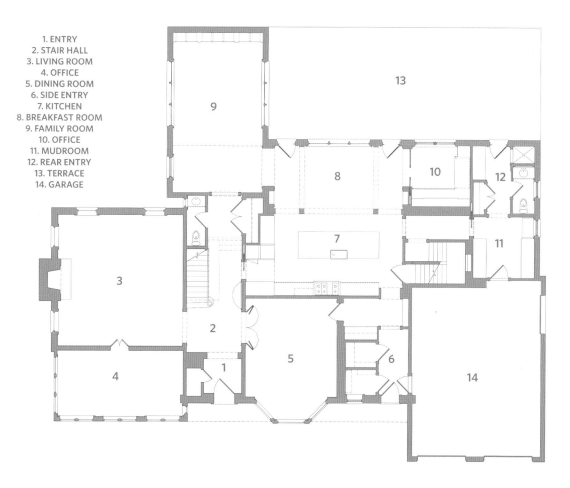

1. ENTRY
2. STAIR HALL
3. LIVING ROOM
4. OFFICE
5. DINING ROOM
6. SIDE ENTRY
7. KITCHEN
8. BREAKFAST ROOM
9. FAMILY ROOM
10. OFFICE
11. MUDROOM
12. REAR ENTRY
13. TERRACE
14. GARAGE

First floor plans before (top) and after (bottom) the addition.

Top: **Street elevation before additions.**
Bottom: **Street elevation after additions.**

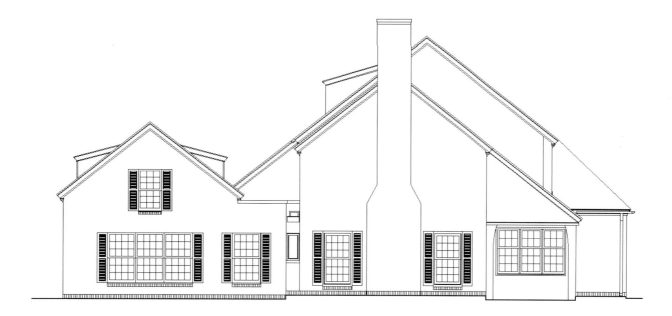

Top: **South side elevation before additions and remodeling**
Bottom: **South side elevation with modifications of existing family room.**

West elevations (top) before and after (bottom) addition.

West elevation after the addition.

Entry and stair hall looking into remodeled family room.

Left: New kitchen looking into breakfast room with connection to family room. Above: Cabinetry in new butler's pantry.

New principal bathrooom.

Knit Together

View of addition from back yard. Porch with dormer for tub alcove above.

This handsome French country house was built in 1959 by the current owner's parents, who worked closely with their architect, Ralph Huszagh, on the design. Traveling through Normandy looking for inspiration, they brought back photographs to communicate to their architect what they wanted the house to look like. The current owner, their daughter, is an interior designer with wonderful collections of furniture and objects. She wanted to remodel the kitchen, enlarge and remodel the principal bedroom suite directly above the existing kitchen, and create a second-floor connection to the unused space over the garage. The garage was given a shed dormer to create livable space, a bathroom, and a stair to the outside connecting down to the swimming pool area. This space was to serve as a guest suite with its own exterior entrance, as well as doubling as a home office. It was connected to the second floor of the house by a passageway constructed over the existing breezeway. The open breezeway continued to access the side door to the kitchen and connect to the pool area from the front of the house.

The owner collects blue ceramics, and she selected a blue picture tile along with a dark blue enameled French cooker for her French country kitchen. These selections and the existing house drove the aesthetic choices. The character, trim, beaming, and paneling in the existing breakfast area was carried into the design of the adjacent kitchen. The existing back bathroom located adjacent to the side entry restricted the working area of the existing kitchen. It was relocated to make for a better layout and a provide space for a kitchen island. The kitchen was opened to the breakfast room, which was provided with French doors out to a covered dining area offering views to the yard. This covered porch was under the expanded second floor principal bedroom suite. In the space created on the second floor, the owner also wanted a larger walk-in closet and a larger compartmented bathroom. The tub occupies a roof dormer with a view of the back yard.

Previous pages: Dormer and stair at side of garage are new additions.

1. ENTRY PORCH
2. ENTRY
3. LIVING ROOM
4. LIBRARY
5. FAMILY ROOM
6. DINING ROOM
7. KITCHEN
8. BREAKFAST ROOM
9. MUDROOM
10. PANTRY
11. BREEZE-WAY
12. GARAGE

1. COVERED PORCH
2. ENTRY
3. LIVING ROOM
4. LIBRARY
5. FAMILY ROOM
6. DINING ROOM
7. KITCHEN
8. BREAKFAST ROOM
9. COVERED PORCH
10. BUTLER'S PANTRY
11. BREEZE-WAY
12. GARAGE

Plans before (top) and after (bottom) the addition.

Additions at left and right sides of house seen from pool area. New shed dormer over garage on the left and porch with new bathroom above on the right.

Following Pages: The new covered porch.

Above: **New kitchen seen from breakfast room.** Right: **Detail of hood and French made range.**

Above: View into breakfast room with new French doors to covered porch. Right: Tub alcove in dormer.

Queen Anne Redux

While not a project that involved an addition, this remodeling represents a way of thinking about altering the exterior and interior of an existing house whose forms and details had been compromised by earlier work.

Awkwardly renovated in the 1980s, with a family room added to the back of the house, the exterior was given ill-proportioned postmodern elements. We replanned the interior of the house to interconnect the house's main space. The details and interior trim were reinvented versions of what was left in a few of the unremodeled parts of the house. The front porch and entry were redesigned, and a column made to match the existing front columns was added to try and regularize the porch's bay spacing. The front porch balusters were also replaced with simple square ones at a closer spacing.

The existing addition was retained but its exterior along with the back of the house was redesigned to incorporate elements that recall those of the existing house including a new "Palladian Window" on the third floor like the one at the front of the house. The family room addition had two steps down from the adjacent kitchen. These went almost the full width of the family room and the new owner felt they were a tripping hazard. The floor was raised to the kitchen level and the existing flat ceiling was removed to extend the space upward to the bottom of the existing collar ties of the original roof framing. In the entry hall, the bench and wall paneling turned out to be a later addition to the house, but one that was poorly integrated into the adjacent stair. This was "tweaked" to make the new bottom stair treads better integrate into the surface of the bench. The stair stringer and stair treads had been painted and to further tie all these elements together the paneling behind the bench and the bench's front were painted.

Because the kitchen was located behind the family room addition, its only exterior wall faced a house a few feet away. With

House with 1980s addition before remodeling.

the sink moved to the island, there was no need for a tall window along this side of the kitchen. To bring in light from the side, we introduced horizontal awning windows. These are not visible from either the street or the backyard. Under the glass fronted upper cabinets we introduced horizontal awning windows that are not visible from either the street or the back yard.

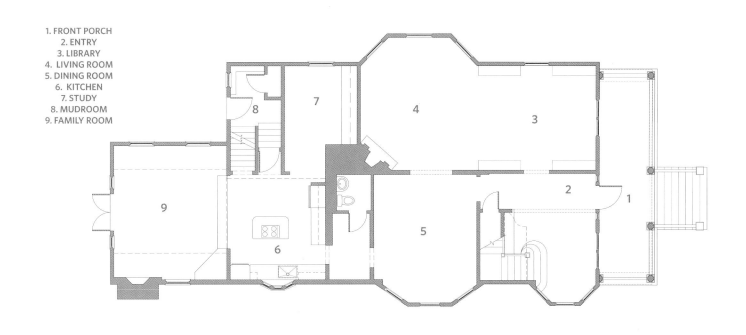

1. FRONT PORCH
2. ENTRY
3. LIBRARY
4. LIVING ROOM
5. DINING ROOM
6. KITCHEN
7. STUDY
8. MUDROOM
9. FAMILY ROOM

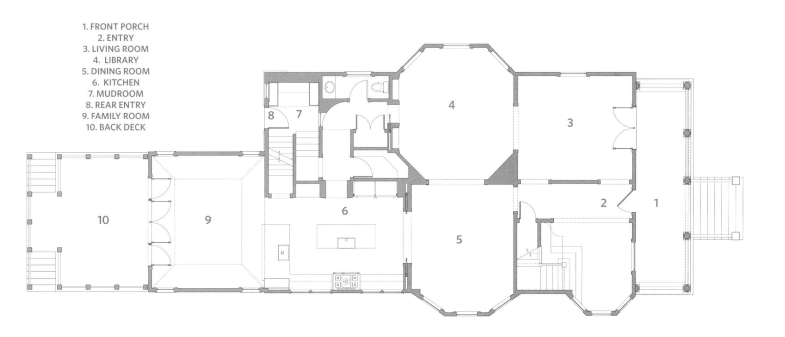

1. FRONT PORCH
2. ENTRY
3. LIVING ROOM
4. LIBRARY
5. DINING ROOM
6. KITCHEN
7. MUDROOM
8. REAR ENTRY
9. FAMILY ROOM
10. BACK DECK

Plans before (top) and after (bottom) the addition.

Before (above) and after (right) views of the front of the house.

Before (above) and after (right) views of staircase and entry hall.

Left: Kitchen seen from family room with pocketing French doors to dining room. Above: Kitchen looking into family room.
Following pages: Family room with French doors to new raised deck.

Principal bathroom. Shower room on the right. French door to closet and dressing room.

First Addition

The addition of a new ground floor living space, with an expansion of the principal bedroom above, is a "first addition" to a house we designed for the same home owner in 1995. The owner, trained as an interior designer and now a studio artist, wanted to add on to the back. The façade, which she wanted to expand, had a symmetrical double gabled roof with an all glass breakfast room centered below. The breakfast room had a flat roof, which was an outside deck serving the principal bedroom.

We felt that there was a problem extending the house. Not only did we not want to destroy the symmetry of the back, but we worried about draining water from the roof between the double gables. We told our client that we couldn't add onto her house. Her response was, "I intend to do an addition and if you won't do it, I'll find someone else." Horrified at the thought that our design might be ruined by another architect, we took the job.

The existing house has divided light casement windows, and our client asked that the new spaces have large undivided windows to better take advantage of the pastoral views of the protected wetlands and forest behind the house. These were a part of a wetland conservancy and were much of the original appeal of the property, guaranteeing that the view from the back of the house to the west would remain an unbuilt prairie. Our addition strategy was to rebuild the breakfast bay and extend the east gabled volume to create the addition. On the ground floor in the new room, the large areas of fixed glass are flanked by divided light French doors with a row of divided light transoms above, designed to mitigate the scale shift from the windows in the existing house. The project also involved the reconstruction of the raised stone terrace behind the house. We were able to add a first-floor covered porch along the west side of the house as a defined exterior space open to the terrace and to provide sun screening on the southwest.

Front of house.

Back of house with original breakfast room.

The new porch mirrors the colonnade, roof, and eave line of the porch off the house's dining room. In this very large addition to a medium sized shingle style house, we felt that matching the materials and details of the existing residence would help keep the addition from looking "a tail trying to wag a dog."

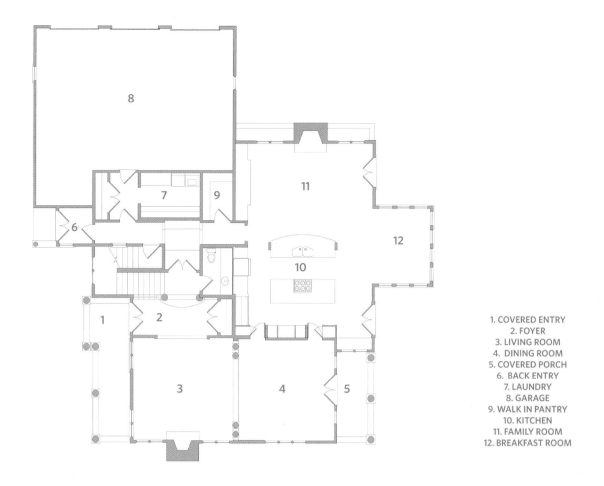

1. COVERED ENTRY
2. FOYER
3. LIVING ROOM
4. DINING ROOM
5. COVERED PORCH
6. BACK ENTRY
7. LAUNDRY
8. GARAGE
9. WALK IN PANTRY
10. KITCHEN
11. FAMILY ROOM
12. BREAKFAST ROOM

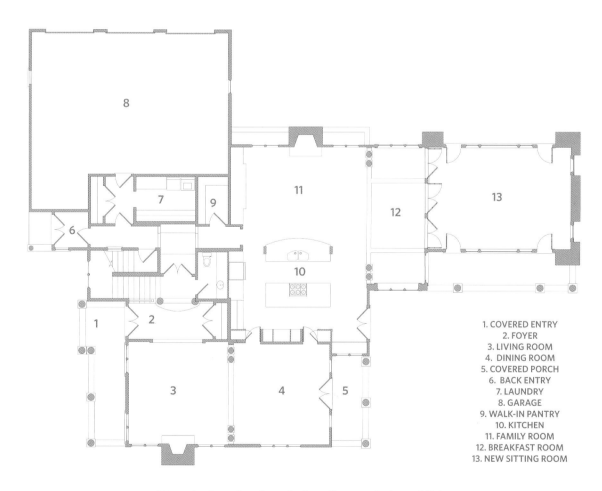

1. COVERED ENTRY
2. FOYER
3. LIVING ROOM
4. DINING ROOM
5. COVERED PORCH
6. BACK ENTRY
7. LAUNDRY
8. GARAGE
9. WALK-IN PANTRY
10. KITCHEN
11. FAMILY ROOM
12. BREAKFAST ROOM
13. NEW SITTING ROOM

Plans before (top) and after (bottom) the addition.

Side view of the house.
Addition is on the right.

Above: View from living room to stair hall and back hallway. Right: Living room. Handmade fireplace tiles were made by the owner. Following pages: Kitchen. Painting in alcove is by owner.

Original family room looking into the new addition. Paired columns repeat from original two-story living room.

View of doors to new
sitting room addition.

New sitting room addition with view to protected wetlands.

Contextual House

In over forty years of residential practice, we have designed only a handful of new houses. Over the years of our practice, working on great older houses has informed our practice. We've come to understand how to build well and to think of millwork and trim as visual systems. This work has informed the way we approach the design of new houses. We also bring to these houses our appreciation of the free plans of Le Corbusier and the spatial importance of columns screens and free standing columns when exposed. Well-budgeted new houses are what most residential practices aspire to, but we have found building house additions both more challenging and, in a sense, easier because they are never as open-ended as the design of a new house. The inclusion of this new house in a book about house additions is intended to bring the ideas presented here full circle from what began as an idea about urban additions to ones about architectural. We conceived the house, illustrated here, as an addition to the 1930s enclave of houses it was designed to relate to.

Charles Hemphill was a residential developer who built houses for the upper middle class along Chicago's Northshore suburbs in the decades before and just after the Second World War. Milburn Park, the site of this new house, is in Evanston, Illinois, just north of the Northwestern University campus and just east of Sheridan Road along the lakefront. Built between 1937 and 1939, Hemphill built eight houses of Wisconsin Lannon stone in Tudor Revival and Colonial Revival styles. All but the three houses facing the lake were sited around an open green with their front entries facing this shared space. The houses on the green all had attached garages accessed by a private driveway at their rear. The shared green space between the fronts of the houses terminates in a row of three houses which face the lake. These houses all have riparian rights. Hemphill's architect, Raymond Houlihan, designed all but

two of the houses, a 1950s ranch house on the lake and the 1950s red brick Colonial that our client took down. The Hemphill houses, some built for clients, but mostly built for sale, offered a design variety within a narrow palette of materials. The roofs were either slate or wood shingles. All the houses but one were faced with buff colored stone. All had divided light casement windows, and all had decorative cut stone elements, most notably carved stone front door surrounds. All the front doors were dark stained wood.

The house that came down was red brick, had eight-foot ceilings, no distinguished interior details, and only one small picture window at the east end of the living room facing the lake. The entry hall was narrow with the stair parallel to the front door. The view upon entering the house was the ascending stairs rather than the lake. Everything visually announced that even though it sat on prime real estate, this was an undistinguished 1950s house with millwork and cabinets that looked like they came from a local lumber yard.

The front of the house we designed was stone with a classical cut stone entry canopy, a stained walnut front door, and casement windows. While the front of the house was stone to relate to the Hemphill houses, the back was done in wood siding in a style we referred to as "classic beach house."

The entry hall is separated from the living dining area by a column screen. The kitchen and family room open to a large, screened porch. At the front of the house, the stair, which ascends from the entry hall, has a built-in bench at its landing. The landing is expressed as a two-sided glass volume at the house's southwest corner. It brings light into the second-floor hallway, serving the secondary bedrooms. The stairs arrive at a two-story high sitting area with a vaulted ceiling. From this space, a second stair continues up to a third-floor guest suite with wonderful views of the lake. The back

"Beach House" side viewed over dune grass from the water.

of the house on the first floor is all windows facing the lake. The house was designed with all the main rooms having lake views except the mudroom and secondary bathrooms. The principal bedroom opens out to a narrow sitting balcony cut into the volume of the back of the house. In the principal bathroom, the toilet room has a view of the lake, as does the sink area through a window above the double vanity. This side of the house, because of the shape of the property, also has views of the water across their neighbor's backyard.

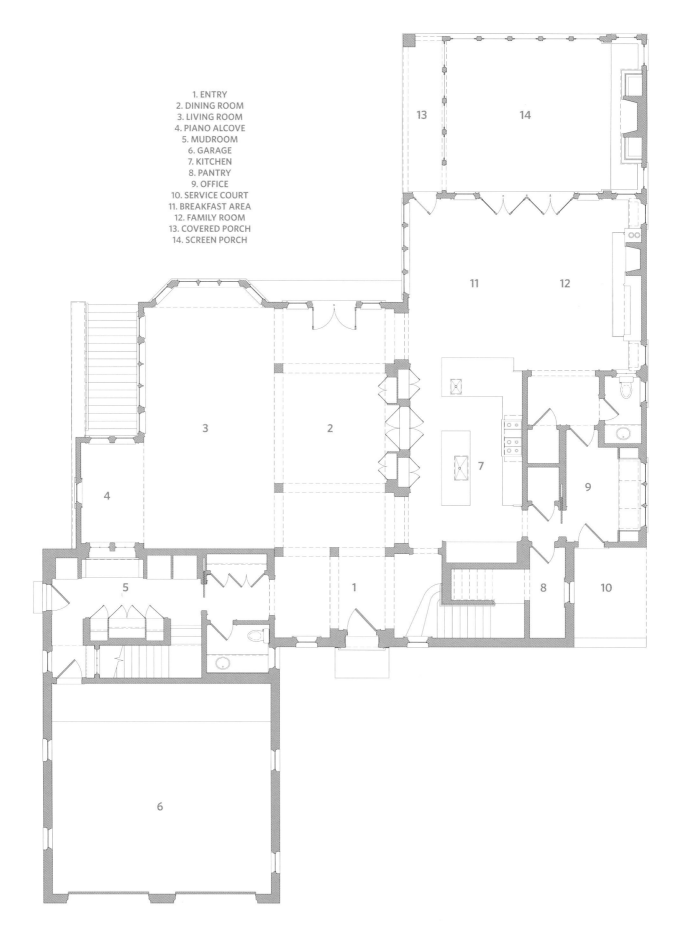

1. ENTRY
2. DINING ROOM
3. LIVING ROOM
4. PIANO ALCOVE
5. MUDROOM
6. GARAGE
7. KITCHEN
8. PANTRY
9. OFFICE
10. SERVICE COURT
11. BREAKFAST AREA
12. FAMILY ROOM
13. COVERED PORCH
14. SCREEN PORCH

First floor plan.

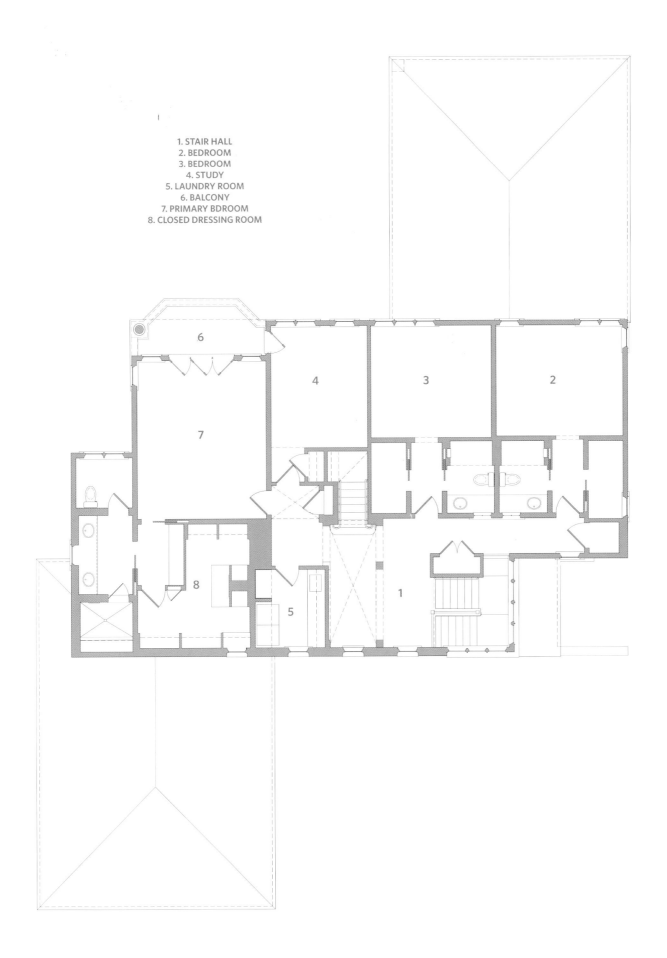

1. STAIR HALL
2. BEDROOM
3. BEDROOM
4. STUDY
5. LAUNDRY ROOM
6. BALCONY
7. PRIMARY BDROOM
8. CLOSED DRESSING ROOM

Second floor plan.

253

Above: Piano alcove at back of living room. Right: Dining area with two-sided glass cabinet also accessible from the kitchen. View into the family room on the left.

Kitchen open to
family room.

Following pages:
Breakfast area
in family room
looking into
living room.

257

Above: Sitting area at second floor stair landing. Right: Stair to third floor guest suite.

Principal bedroom and balcony.

Principal bathroom with
French door to toilet room
with a view of the lake.

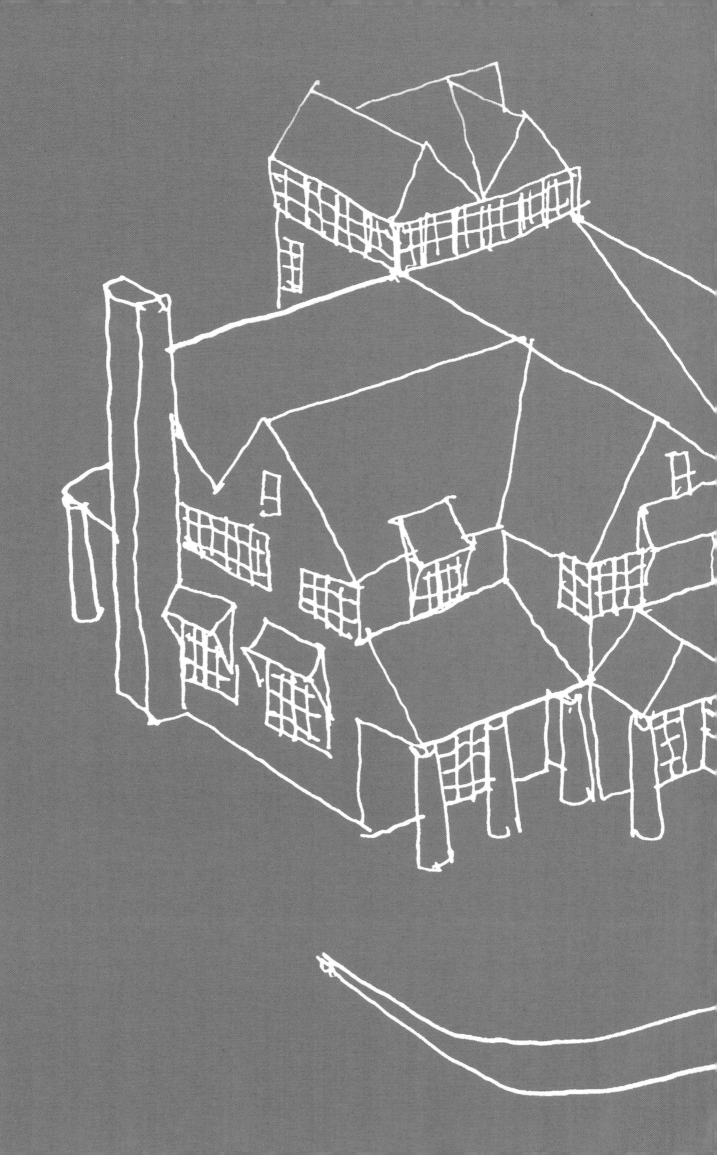

Concept Drawings

(1986-2023)

Drawing is the primary skill set for architects. Drawings communicate everything from the conceptualization of a project to the detailed instructions for its realization. Drawings fall roughly into two main categories. They are either pictorial, trying to show how a building is intended to look, or they are analytic. Analytic drawings explain all of the internal and external relationships of a building's design and convey the concept for a building's spatial organization, composition, and proportions. Analytic drawings can be diagrams but typically they are plans, sections, and exterior and interior elevations. None of these drawings show us buildings as we see them, rather they show us the ideas that visually organize the spaces and the surfaces that comprise a building.

The drawings in this book are a way to understand the projects, providing information about design relationships often not shown in photographs. Every project in this book is accompanied by analytic drawings. Complete before and after floor plans are included, even when the addition and remodeling is small, because it is important to understand the existing house as the context for the new work. This context is the internal and external organization of the existing home. The inclusion of before and after elevation drawings also explain changes in the absence of good photographs taken before work began. Elevation drawings, like floor plans, also show ideas about the composition of a house's massing, roof forms, and wall openings.

Freehand drawings and sketches are also an important part of the conceptual design of any project. Loosely sketched floor plans and sketches on the back of napkins are interesting when they show the development of planning that is in flux. These "napkin sketches," as they are often called, are most interesting when they show the early presence of an idea or building form that persists to become the building as built. Alvar Aalto's published

sketches or those of Alvaro Siza are remarkable in that way. The design drawings included here were done as part of the development of the design. They were a way to consider alternate versions of how things could look, not just to show to clients. Making drawings are an important way to represent what we see in our mind's eye. In our additions, exteriors are often examined in small doodled axonometric sketches seen from above. These sketches study building massing, roof forms, and window openings. Interior spaces are developed in perspectives with very wide-angle views—often with multiple vanishing points—showing not only the field of vision the eye can see but what the mind sees. The thumbnail interior perspectives by Le Corbusier are memorable examples of this way of drawing.

Many of the photographs in this book were taken to replicate the imagined views shown in the following pages.

Previous pages: Back of house with addition. See pages 232-233.

Mudroom desk with door to kitchen. See page 91.

Breakfast area. See page 92.

Closet and dressing area (not photographed.)
Space is through French door opposite tub. See page 123.

Kitchen. See pages 180-181.

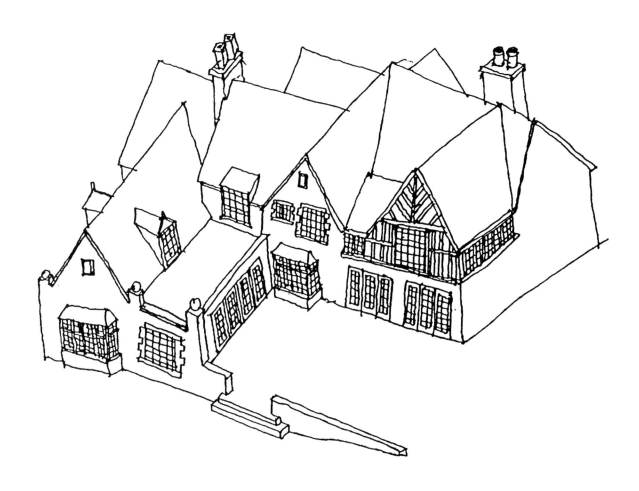

Family room and second floor bedroom addition. See pages 156-161.

New bathroom addition. See pages 138-139.

Top: Bathroom. See pages 184-185.
Bottom: Bathroom. See page 265.

Axonometric and elevation study. See pages 243-243

Acknowledgements

The impetus for this book was Julie Hacker's desire to document the work of Cohen & Hacker since the publication of *Transforming the Traditional: The Work of Cohen & Hacker Architects* in 2009. This work has been primarily additions and remodeling, hence the current volume. Many years ago, Judith Neisser, who wrote about art and architecture for *Chicago Magazine* wanted to write about our house additions. "I have the perfect title," she said, "First Additions."

The work shown in this book was realized through the efforts of our talented staff, primarily Paul Billingsley, Brad Korando, Olga Borofsky, Amy Scruggs, Nicole Ducar, Steve Liska, Gary Shumaker, and John Jacobs. Our thanks also to the other architects who have worked with us over the past two decades. Some of the projects in "Modest Beginnings" were done with Anders Nerim, a partner in the mid-1970s, who was important to the early work of our firm. Thanks to Josh Puce, who prepared most of the drawings in this book from the demolition plans, floor plans, and elevations in archived sets of construction drawings. The article, "On Adding On" and its illustrations is reproduced as it appeared in *Thresholds* (University of Illinois School of Architecture, Rizzoli), however the text was reset in a typeface to match that used for this book.

I would like to thank Christian Bjone and Steven Hurtt, who read and commented on portions of the text. Christian Bjone also provided the drawings for our "Classical Screen Porch Addition" (p. 45), which he made in the late 1970s. This publication is also the work of Mike Williams, a partner in CityFiles Press and a talented book designer, who saw a book in what began as a collection of academic essays, drawings, and photographs. We want to thank Mike for his patience working with a client who wanted to micromanage the layout of almost every page.

We have been fortunate over the years to work with talented residential contractors who have built our projects beautifully. We have learned from them, and they have often been collaborators. Our thanks to Bob Compher of C&P Remodeling, Matthew Kurtyka of Windsor Builders, Arthur G. Nelson Inc., Steve Sturm of Sturm Builders, Lynch Construction, and Michael Mariottini of Mariottini Construction, who built most of the projects shown in this book. Our cabinetry designs were executed to impeccable standards by Paoli Woodworking.

We would like to acknowledge the following interior designers who were responsible for furniture, rugs, window coverings, and decorative lighting fixtures shown on the pages listed below.

Stephanie Wolhner Design, pp. 118-133, 172-189.

Pam Maher Design, pp. 82-93.

Michael Abrams Interiors, pp. 106-117.

Lauren Coburn LLC, pp. 146-155.

SuzAnn Kleitzien Design, pp. 216-29.

jamesthomas LLC, pp. 246-265.

Where not credited, furnishings are by the homeowners. All cabinetry and architectural interiors were designed by Cohen & Hacker.

Left:. **View from butlers' pantry into addition. See pages 54-63.**

Photo Credits

Almost all the photographs in this book are by three photographers, Jon Miller of Hedrich Blessing, Dave Burk of Hedrich Blessing, and more recently by Tony Soluri Photography. Two of the projects published here were photographed by VHT Studios. The photographs in "Modest Beginnings" are by Cohen & Hacker as well as the photographs of houses taken before they were altered.

Jon Miller-Hedrich Blessing: pp. 82-93, 105-114, 127-133, 146-147, 150-154, 156-157, 153-165, 166-171, 178-189, 232.

Dave Burk-Hedrich Blessing: pp. 216-217, 220, 223-225, 228-229, 246-265.

Tony Soluri Photography: pp. 54-63, 64-81, 118-121, 134-145, 172-173, 176-177, 204-215, 230-231, 234-245.

VHT Studios: pp. 94-104, 190-191, 197-203, 288-219, 222.

Dustin Halleck Photography: pp. 226-227.

Scott Shigley Photography: pp. 115-116.

Left: New mudroom. See pages 216-229.

ORO Editions
Publishers of Architecture, Art, and Design
Gordon Goff: Publisher

www.oroeditions.com
info@oroeditions.com

Published by ORO Editions

Author: Stuart Cohen and Julie Hacker
Book Design: Michael Williams
Project Manager: Jake Anderson

10 9 8 7 6 5 4 3 2 1 First Edition

ISBN: 978-1-961856-16-5

Prepress and Print work by ORO Editions Inc
Printed in China

ORO Editions makes a continuous effort to minimize the overall carbon footprint of its publications. As part of this goal, ORO, in association with Global ReLeaf, arranges to plant trees to replace those used in the manufacturing of the paper produced for its books. Global ReLeaf is an international campaign run by American Forests, one of the world's oldest nonprofit conservation organizations. Global ReLeaf is American Forests' education and action program that helps individuals, organizations, agencies, and corporations improve the local and global environment by planting and caring for trees.

Dust jacket photos:
Front cover: Jon Miller-Hedrich Blessing
Back cover: Tony Soluri Photography
Front flap: Tony Soluri Photography
Back flap: Melissa Pinney